D0735575

LIVING PROOF
Telling Your Story
to Make a Difference
EXPANDED EDITION

Praise for
Living Proof: Telling Your Story to Make a Difference

"As authentic as an advocate's story may be ...it can always be improved in style and delivery; that's the mission of this exceptional instructional guide. ... Smart, well-delivered, and timely advice to help advocates and spokespersons tell the most effective stories."
Kirkus Reviews

"If we're going to make change, we're going to have to tell our stories and tell them effectively. This book shows us how."
Paul Loeb, author of *Soul of a Citizen*

"*Living Proof* had a fantastic impact on my students. Rarely have I seen students so enthusiastically engaged with a required course text. They learned about the impact of transforming personal experience into public action. The exercises in the text offered excellent insight and created a platform for one of the best semesters I have ever had with this course."
Dr. Michael Tew, Professor of Communication, Director of the Center for the Study of Equality and Human Rights, Eastern Michigan University

"Everyone's talking about the power of stories these days but we need more resources to help advocates, activists, and nonprofit communicators find their own voices, get heard, and win real change. *Living Proof* is a sourcebook for trainers and advocates alike that fills that need. It's full of hands-on exercises, good ideas, and useful suggestions."
Gordon Mayer, National People's Action

"The principles of rhetoric are translated here into contemporary language to make them accessible to anyone who wants to persuade through storytelling. This book provides instructions, examples, and exercises to make your stories come alive. A superb guide."

Dr. Sonja K. Foss, University of Colorado Denver, author of *Contemporary Perspectives on Rhetoric* and *Inviting Transformation: Presentational Speaking for a Changing World*

"As a longtime radio journalist and adversity-driven advocate, I've spent years attempting to hone my storytelling skills. This book, more than any other I've run across, succeeds in consolidating and bringing to life those very skills in one powerful primer. *Living Proof* communicates so well the art of communication!"

Jeff Bell, author of *Rewind, Replay, Repeat: A Memoir of OCD*

"This is an extraordinarily effective guide for advocates seeking all kinds of social and institutional change. But don't mistake it for another 'how to.' Above all, this book helps us to see how to take our lives seriously enough to tell them. The practices recommended in this book are a gift. A great read for all interested in what their stories can do for others."

Dr. Della Pollock, The University of North Carolina at Chapel Hill, author of *Telling Bodies Performing Birth* and editor of *Remembering: Oral History Performance*

John Capecci and Timothy Cage

Living PROOF

Telling Your Story to Make a Difference

Expanded Edition

Granville Circle
— P R E S S —

Published by
Granville Circle Press
2811 University Ave. SE #14445
Minneapolis, MN 55414

Printed in the United States of America and
distributed by Itasca Books www.itascabooks.com
1-800-901-3480

Instructor Resources. Study guides and additional classroom materials are available at livingproofadvocacy.com/blog/resources.

Quantity sales. Discounts are available on quantity purchases. For details, contact the publisher at sales@granvillecirclepress.com.

Orders for course adoption. Review copies are available by contacting sales@granvillecirclepress.com. To order for course adoption, contact the distributor at orders@itascabooks.com.

Excerpt from *The Story of Your Life* by Tristine Rainer. Copyright 1998 by Tristine Rainer. Reprinted by permission of the author.

Excerpt from "New Beginning," by LeDerick Horne. Reprinted by permission of the author.

Excerpts from *Soul of a Citizen* by Paul Loeb. Copyright 1999, 2010 by Paul Loeb. Reprinted by permission of the author.

Excerpts from *The Story Handbook: A Primer on Language and Storytelling for Land Conservationists.* Copyright 2003 by The Trust for Public Land. Reprinted by permission of the publisher.

Excerpt from *It Was Like a Fever: Storytelling in Protest and Politics* by Francesca Polletta. Copyright 2006, University of Chicago Press. Reprinted by permission of the publisher.

This Granville Circle Press book is printed on paper that contains 30% post-consumer fiber with FSC certification, manufactured using biogas energy. Printers are powered by energy harnessed on the wind farms of southwestern Minnesota.

ISBN: 978-0-9838703-4-0

Library of Congress Cataloging-in-Publication Data
2015906793

Capecci, John.
Living proof : telling your story to make a difference / John Capecci and Timothy Cage.
Minneapolis, MN : Granville Circle Press, c2015.
p. cm.
1. Public speaking—Handbooks, manuals, etc. 2. Social advocacy—Handbooks, manuals, etc.
3. Social justice—Handbooks, manuals, etc. 4. Nonprofit organizations—Public relations.
I. Cage, Timothy. II. Title.
PN4129.15 .C34 2012   808.51

Cover, interior design and illustrations—Brad Norr, www.bradnorrdesign.com
Editor—Christianne Thillen
Indexer—Dianna Haught
Photos, LeadingAge Kansas, Brian Killion

DEDICATION

To the thousands of advocates whose stories we've been privileged to share, and in memory of those whose stories continue to inspire us:

Gianna Capecci
Robert Compitello
Deborah Voss Mankiewicz
Annie Lewis Martin

Contents

Living Proof Exercises

Introduction to the Expanded Edition

Everybody likes ice cream, right?

That's the bet Ocean Robbins made as he stood before an audience of five hundred and told his story.

My grandfather started Baskin-Robbins ice cream company. Thirty-one flavors. (Audience applauds.) And from his earliest childhood, my dad, John Robbins, was groomed to one day join his father in the family company. He grew up with an ice cream cone-shaped swimming pool in the backyard and a commercial freezer in the garage, full of thirty-one flavors of ice cream at all times. He grew up working in the factory and he was expected to join the family business. But then, when he was in his early 20s, he was offered that chance and he said "no." And my grandfather was pretty hurt and said "Why? What has come over you?" And my dad said, "You know, dad, we live in a world under a nuclear shadow. Every two seconds another child is dying of hunger and malnutrition. The environment's deteriorating rapidly under the impact of human activity. And given those circumstances . . . I don't think inventing a thirty-second flavor is an adequate response for my life.

Ocean delivered this keynote address at the National Alliance for Peace conference in Washington, DC. A tireless advocate for young people building a better world, he drew upon his experience to talk about citizen responsibility and youth empowerment. He hooked the audience with his unique family history. And he told his personal story naturally and passionately.

While writing *Living Proof* and since its initial publication in 2012, we've been fortunate to meet many people like Ocean who've found they can make a real difference telling their personal stories. Working for more than twenty years as communication trainers, we've helped thousands reach that same goal. Some, like Ocean, tell their stories on a national stage; many more share their stories in community meetings or with bloggers and local newspaper reporters. They're "ordinary" people and first-time speakers. They're also skilled presenters and media personalities. They speak in support of large and small nonprofits, local and national groups and publicity campaigns for the arts, the environment, education, health, and youth. They stand at lecterns, sit in circles, and knock on doors. They're interviewed over the phone and on-camera. They've appeared in high-school gymnasiums, at the White House, and on TV talk shows. But no matter where they're from or how much (or how little) experience they have, these people share the same objective: to tell a personal story with clarity, passion and purpose, and to have that story make a difference for someone or some cause. They are advocates.

In Roman law, the *advocatus* was called to plead others' cases in a court of law. Today, our use of the word *advocate* has expanded beyond the legal sense to include anyone who supports or recommends a cause, policy, or practice—anyone working to make the world a better place. We wrote *Living Proof* for these many people because we've seen how, with the right support and coaching, ordinary people can become extraordinary advocates.

Personal stories have a unique ability to affect audiences. But it's not by story alone that successful advocates urge others to take action, whether that action is donating money, improving public policy, or changing behavior. Advocating

> **It's not by story alone that successful advocates urge others to take action.**

with stories takes a specific kind of preparation. It requires practice with elements of persuasion, public speaking, media interview skills and storytelling—not to mention healthy doses of fortitude and commitment.

We also wrote *Living Proof* to provide advocates with a single resource for this special kind of preparation—a one-stop shop that gathers together what you need to stand up next week and tell your story effectively at a town meeting or on national television. We knew from experience that such a book didn't exist. In fact, shortly after the initial publication of *Living Proof*, an advocate told us that whenever she had gone looking for a book that focused on the power of stories, she was directed to Robert McKee's *Story: Style, Structure, Substance, and the Principles of Screenwriting*—a classic text on the craft of storytelling, but one that's focused on screenwriting, not advocacy. When participants in our workshops had asked for additional resources, we too could only point them to excellent works like McKee's or other writings about personal narratives, public speaking, media skills, persuasion, marketing, autobiography, civic action, and social change. There was no single, accessible guidebook that pulled together the essentials and specifically focused on how one person tells a personal story in this unique context—as an advocate.

Living Proof is based on our experiences training advocates, and it draws from the work of experts and colleagues in many fields. It focuses on the essentials: what you need to know to tell your story effectively in public (from talks to keynotes) and media interviews (from blogs to broadcast). At the center are **The Five Qualities of the Well-Told Advocacy Story** (page 33). These qualities form a simple, strong foundation for success, wherever and whenever you tell your stories. You'll find the Five Qualities echoed throughout *Living Proof.*

This edition of *Living Proof* follows the same general progression as the previous edition, though now it's expanded into two parts: Part One, Preparing to Make a Difference, explores the power of stories, recommends ways of finding, crafting, and preparing your stories, and introduces the skills needed to deliver powerful presentations and give great media interviews. Part Two, Telling Your Story, contains two new chapters that explore barriers you may encounter as you prepare to go public, and how advocacy acts as a persuasive agent of social change. Part Two also includes chapters that offer tips and tools for a variety of public speaking and interview situations.

You can work through *Living Proof* from start to finish—over a weekend, a week, or in conjunction with a course of study. You can also flip to the sections most useful to you right now or keep the book on hand as a resource. As in our workshops, we've tried to make *Living Proof* adaptable to individual needs.

- Each chapter's opening page previews what's inside.
- *Exercises* help you explore and plan.
- *Practice Runs* guide your run-throughs for specific speaking engagements or interviews.
- *Prep Sheets* provide blank forms to plan your talk or interview.
- Sidebars feature additional notes from us, insights from advocates, and inspiration from experts.

Since the publication of the first edition of *Living Proof*, we've trained and advised many new advocates and organizations working on causes as diverse as sustainable agricultural practices, lung cancer, community bicycling programs, racial and gender equity, and safer teen driving. We've also talked with instructors, trainers, and change makers who are applying *Living Proof* principles in their classrooms, in communications and marketing efforts, in community organizing, and in fundraising campaigns. This expanded edition of *Living Proof* allows us to share some of the insights we've gained in conversations with our readers and to include additional information appropriate to specific contexts. In this new edition of *Living Proof*, you'll find:

- Refinements and expansions to certain topics such as "pointing to the positive" and "framing"
- New examples from advocates and organizations
- Additional suggestions on how to structure talks or presentations
- New sections that explore advocacy, persuasion, social change, and the barriers you may encounter as you prepare to speak out

Oh, and we've added a bit more white space to the design of the print edition since so many readers told us they like to write in the margins.

We've also taken the opportunity with this new edition to clarify a few key themes:

This is about spoken communication. While *advocacy* can mean letter writing or voting or tweeting, in *Living Proof* we honor the classical root of the word and focus specifically on public speech: from casual talks to formal presentations to interactions with the media. While the principles in *Living*

> The Latin root of *advocate* is *vocare* (to call), closely related to *vox* (voice).

Proof are certainly applicable to written or visual forms of advocacy and storytelling, our focus here is on respectful and effective face-to-face communication.

Advocacy is a persuasive act that benefits others. When you speak as an advocate telling a personal story, you do so with a purpose. You are asking others to *do something* as a result of hearing your experience. You hope others will relate to, connect with and perhaps be moved by your story—but it is always with the aim that that connection will lead to some positive action that will benefit others. Our recommendations throughout *Living Proof* for crafting, structuring, framing and delivering stories always place storytelling within this context of altruistic persuasive communication. We explore this stance further in Chapter 12, Public Speech, Public Narrative.

This is (often) about cultural change. It's perhaps obvious— but no less important to state—that we view personal stories as powerful instruments of both individual and cultural change. Personal stories are always in dialogue with larger cultural narratives, either helping to build them, strengthen them or—as is often the case—challenging and rewriting them to more accurately reflect a better, more just reality. We explore this notion also in Chapter 12.

This is more about the *how* and the *why* than it is the *what*. *Living Proof* is not about fitting your life story into an existing story structure, nor finding the "best type" of advocacy story. That's because we define effective advocacy stories in context, by how well they stand as proof of an idea or cause—not by independent qualities of what makes a "good" story such as drama, a sense of struggle or high emotional content. Advocacy requires personal stories of all kinds. That's why you'll find examples in *Living Proof* that range from Gayathri Ramprasad's heart-rending story of her consuming depression, when her husband discovered her in the backyard trying to dig her own grave, to Teresa Opheim's quiet reflection on the importance of family farming, describing the gradual erasure of her grandparents' farm from the Iowa landscape.

> "Americans have always loved outlaws, but the true heroes are likely to be in-laws and the other good people who help us travel through our lives. ... right now our country desperately needs just such people to step up to the plate and try to make things better."[2]
>
> **—Mary Pipher**

Throughout *Living Proof* you'll meet advocates like Gayathri and Teresa, from diverse walks of life, with stories big and small. These advocates have generously shared their stories and their experiences with us, and we're indebted to them for the richness they bring to this work.[1] They have reminded us again and again of the simple power of a well-told story and we're thankful for the positive changes they're working toward.

Your stories, too, *can* make a difference. We offer *Living Proof* as a guide. Be an advocate for the people and causes important to you, using the most powerful tool only you have—your personal stories.

John and Tim

You can read about many of the advocates mentioned in *Living Proof* and view videos of their advocacy at www.livingproofadvocacy.com/blog/resources.

Part
ONE

Preparing to Make a Difference

Get Ready

However you work with *Living Proof*—whether you read it from start to finish or flip to the sections that are most relevant to you—be sure to take these important first steps.

- **Complete the first two exercises: My Six-Word Reason and Story Map.** My Six-Word Reason (page 26) is a great starting point that focuses immediately on your goals. Story Map (page 42) is the important conceptual foundation for much of the work in *Living Proof*, and you'll return to it often.

- **Start speaking now.** While you may share your stories in written form online or in print, our focus in *Living Proof* is on the power of the *spoken* story. So speak out early and often. When you talk out your ideas, even stand and speak them alone in your home or office, you're training your body and voice, and this "everyday training" goes a long way in helping you become more comfortable and confident. Of course, there are times when

How To Free-Tell

1. Find a comfortable, private space.

2. Set a timer for 2 minutes.

3. Begin speaking and continue until the time is up. Don't critique yourself or worry that your story is coming out sloppily; free-telling is the verbal equivalent of writing a first draft or doodling. If you get stuck, just repeat the last thing you've said until a new thought comes to mind.

4. If you need to pause and jot down a moment of brilliance, do. But continue speaking immediately. If you can, record your free-telling and then listen for ideas or language you may want to keep in subsequent "drafts."

you need to work out your ideas on paper. That's fine. But don't rely too heavily on the written word. As you get used to speaking your stories, you'll get ever closer to a comfortable and genuine delivery.

- **Practice *free-telling*.** One way to get in the habit of speaking your work is to use *free-telling*, a composition technique based on *free-writing*. Free-writing is a stream-of-consciousness exercise that writers use to generate material and break through writer's block: the writer sets an amount of time (say five or ten minutes) and doesn't stop writing until the time is up. Not all of what is written is usable, but the exercise forces the writer to put on paper whatever comes to mind—often, great ideas that were lurking just under the surface. The principle behind free-telling is the same, and a number of exercises in *Living Proof* recommend this technique. Free-telling is particularly helpful as you search for the parts of your experience that will become your story, as you craft your language, and as you practice for presentations and interviews.

- **Decide how you'll capture your ideas.** Plan how you'll keep notes or record your insights from the exercises in *Living Proof*: a written or electronic journal, an actual or online filing system, or an audio or video recorder.

- **Enlist partners.** Stories need listeners, and speakers need audiences. As you work on your story, it will often take someone saying, "Hey, that's really interesting" or "I'm confused. Tell me more about that" or "Is that detail really necessary?" If you want to measure how your story takes shape or affects others, you'll need a partner or coach. A partner may be another advocate working on the same or different goals or a professional communication coach. Whoever you choose, make sure it's someone who can give you candid and helpful feedback.

- **Go with the flow.** Preparing to tell a personal story publicly rarely follows a straightforward, linear path. It requires giving over to the fluid creative process—that back and forth, push and pull that happens as you craft your experience into stories, adapt to changing settings and audiences, and manage your identity as a public advocate. Be flexible, stay limber. Here we go.

> **Working with a Partner**
>
> Be specific about what you'd like your partner to listen or watch for. Ask open-ended questions that prompt specific responses rather than questions that will get a yes or no answer. You'll get more useful information from "What part of my story can you visualize most clearly?" than from "So, was that okay?"

Chapter 1

Your Stories as Living Proof

IN THIS CHAPTER:

❏ How advocates and organizations use stories
❏ Why and when stories work—and why and when they don't
❏ An important exercise: My Six-Word Reason
❏ Five qualities of the well-told advocacy story

Answering the Call

During a small fundraising event for a cancer-support organization in Minneapolis, Derek Cotton stands in a board member's living room, clutching a half-page of notes. He tells guests what it felt like to be diagnosed with colon cancer and how, when he lived in Texas, the Dallas affiliate of the organization provided support that "balanced me out. Kept me off the ledge."

Loren Vaillancourt takes a deep breath as the news anchor of CBS's The Early Show says, "You believe it was distracted driving that led to your brother's death. He was just 21 years old. What happened in that accident?"

Sitting with other parents in the library of her son's Brooklyn, NY grade school, Theresa Greenleaf calmly explains what it's like being the mom of a kid with food allergies, how appreciative she is of the school's support and assistance— and how critical parents' cooperation is to safeguarding all kids at the school who have allergies or asthma.

Nineteen-year-old college student Zach Wahls hears his name announced in the rotunda of the Iowa House chamber. He walks to the lectern and turns to face the standing-room only crowd of lawmakers and citizens. Hands shaking, he taps the start button on the timer of his

*iPod and sets it down. He has three minutes to make his
case in defense of his family.*

Every day, millions of people go public.

They stand up at community meetings to address their friends and neighbors. They sit under bright lights in a television studio, waiting for the interviewer's next question. They approach lecterns, adjust microphones, and look out at unfamiliar faces.

At rallies and fundraisers, in radio and television studios, in community centers, on the phone with local reporters and in front of web or smartphone cameras, millions of individuals like you come forward daily to tell their stories.

They speak to raise awareness. They speak to change minds. They speak to educate, mobilize, or empower others, to promote a beneficial product or service, and to raise money. They speak for causes local and global—from creating safer schools to reducing the incidence of heart disease, from encouraging arts funding to ending homelessness. They tell their stories with anger, humor, hope, candor, and passion. They go public with their personal and sometimes intimate stories not for their own celebrity—though they may in fact be celebrities—nor purely for dramatic effect, though their stories may be dramatic.

They tell their stories because they believe they can help others and make a difference.

Like you, they are advocates.

Whether you call yourself a spokesperson, activist, representative, change-maker or champion, if you speak out on behalf of someone or some cause, you are an advocate. Advocates fight for the rights of others. Advocates publicly endorse valuable products or services. Advocates raise funds for a cause. In each instance, the action at the heart of advocacy remains the

> **You share an objective with all other advocates: to have your story move audiences from apathy to empathy to action.**

same: speaking out. You are answering the call to help others and—in the true spirit of advocacy—are being vocal about it.

You may have come to advocacy on your own, it may be part of your job or you may have been asked to "put a face" on a campaign by serving as its spokesperson. You may be acting as a lone crusader or as part of a larger advocacy effort. Either way, you share an objective with all other advocates: to have your story move audiences from apathy to empathy to action.

When Derek Cotton told the people gathered in that Minneapolis living room of the support he received from Gilda's Club in Dallas, he was living proof of the value of this national cancer support organization. He advocated for opening a Gilda's Club affiliate in the Twin Cities, his new home. He spoke in support of others dealing with cancer, and he wanted the people in that living room to open their wallets.

When Loren Vaillancourt told the CBS anchor that her brother Kelson was killed in a crash involving a distracted driver, she was living proof of the personal loss that results from a preventable accident. She spoke on behalf of others at risk on the road, and wanted viewers to change their driving behaviors and open their eyes.

When Theresa Greenleaf described to other parents the night her son suffered a severe allergic reaction and collapsed in the cab on the way to the hospital, she was living proof of the importance of vigilance. She advocated for compliance with school policies regarding allergens in packed lunches. She spoke in support of her son and others at the school. She wanted the parents in that school library to open their hearts.

When Zach Wahls, Eagle Scout with two moms, testified before the Iowa House of Representatives in 2011 that "our family really isn't so different from any other Iowa family," he was living proof that loving families come in all forms. He spoke against codifying discrimination. He wanted the legislature and fellow citizens to open their minds.

Like Derek, Loren, Theresa and Zach, you are an advocate because you, too, hope your story can move others to act.

Why Stories Work

There are more than 2.3 million nonprofit organizations in the United States, and the vast majority rely on people like you to share stories and help them deliver their messages.[1] Social movements—from advancing civil rights to working for environmental justice—have been built upon individuals' stories. Commercial businesses, too, depend on the stories of real people to prove the value of a product or service, whether it's a vaccine that saves lives or a light bulb that saves energy. And every day, individuals committed to making a difference in their corners of the world are standing up to say, "Let me tell you what happened. Let me show you what I've seen."

> Google™ **"share your story"** and you'll get millions of responses including the Kansas City Public Library, the Native American Advocacy Program, the Human Rights Campaign, the National Council of La Raza, The National Breast Cancer Foundation, The American Bible Society, Harvard University, Greenpeace and The Alaska Tobacco Control Alliance. The organizations and causes that rely on people like you to share a story are numerous and diverse.

What these diverse groups and individuals have in common is the belief that stories can provide compelling answers to the question: "Why should anyone care?"

Every day we see examples of how one person's story *can* make us care, inspire us, or persuade us to act. An inspirational news feature shows an athlete overcoming her personal challenges to win Olympic gold, and we reevaluate our own goals and motivations. A beloved celebrity talks candidly about his battle with Parkinson's disease and, thinking of friends similarly affected, we make a donation to help fund research. A bereaved mother stands up at a local school board meeting and tells how her son, the victim of a hate crime, was bullied in the school hallways and we change our minds about how safe and inclusive our schools are.

The questions about how and why we respond to personal stories this way constitute a vast field of study that spans anthropology, psychology, theater, ethnography, communication, and folklore, as well as public relations, advertising, and marketing. The power of storytelling is not news.

But some claim we are currently in a "golden age" of story. Storytelling skills are encouraged in MBA and medical training programs, scientific institutions, and law schools. The shelves of our local and online bookstores overflow with guides on how to tell stories to enhance leadership skills, build community, alter our life's direction, create an oral or written personal history for our families, brand our business, and sell more widgets. All these applications are grounded in the same fundamental truth: we are storytelling beings. So when we use our own stories as tools for advocacy, we tap into an essential and universal quality.

The ability to see our lives as stories and share those stories with others is at

The Universal Need for Connection

A study at The Wharton School asked participants to read three stories and contribute $5 to alleviate hunger in Africa. In one version, their donation would go to a specific 7-year-old girl in Mali named Rokia; in the second, to millions of suffering Africans; in the third, to Rokia—but in this version, she was presented within the larger context of world hunger: "Rokia is just one of millions suffering from hunger." The study found that people were more likely to give directly to the story of Rokia—not to anonymous millions and not to Rokia when presented as part of a larger scenario. Stories of individuals draw upon our universal need for connection.[2]

the core of what it means to be human. We use stories to order and make sense of our lives, to define who we are, even to construct our realities: this happened, then this happened, then this. I was, I am, I will be. We recount our dreams, narrate our days, and organize our memories into stories we tell others and ourselves. So, as natural-born storytellers, we respond to others' stories because they are deeply, intimately familiar.

But stories also speak to us differently than other types of communication. If you've ever sat through a mind-numbing "data dump" presentation while a speaker bombards you with statistics and diagrams, you've experienced the hunger for story. Through tears of boredom, you wish with all your heart the speaker would step away from the PowerPoint® of bar graphs and pie charts, look at you, and say, "Let me give you an example of what I mean. On my way to the lecture today . . ." Ah, you'd prick up your ears. Suddenly you're on familiar turf, where abstract ideas become concrete, where knowledge is colored with emotion. Stories invite us into a world of specific sights, feelings, drama, dialogue, and people—not generalities and statistical analyses.

When the stories you tell are from your life, you give audiences an opportunity to feel and imagine with you, to understand

> "Some believe their personal stories don't matter, that others won't care, or that we shouldn't talk about ourselves so much. But if we do public work, we have the responsibility to give a public account of ourselves—where we came from, why we do what we do, and where we think we're going...If we don't author our story, others will—and may tell our story in ways that we may not like."[3]
>
> —**Marshall Ganz, senior lecturer in public policy at the Kennedy School of Government at Harvard University**

in a meaningful way just why they *should* care. The enormity of problems like hunger and social injustice can certainly motivate us to act. We can be convinced logically of the need for intervention and change. But it's very often the story of one individual that ultimately makes the difference—by offering living proof.

When Derek Cotton was asked by Gilda's Club Twin Cities to speak on behalf of the organization and to share what he had experienced at the Dallas affiliate of Gilda's Club (a cancer support organization started by friends of *Saturday Night Live* comedian Gilda Radner), he had never told his cancer story publicly. He says, "When I was asked to tell my story, my first response was, 'I don't think I'm your guy. I don't have this fantastic story to tell. I don't have anything dramatic to say.' I had cancer. I got better."

But the organization knew Derek had an important experience to share with potential donors. Gilda's Club was raising funds to open a "clubhouse" in the twin cities of Minneapolis and Saint Paul. There wasn't yet a building they could point to and say, "This is it. This is what happens here. Support *this*." Because Derek had attended a Gilda's Club when he lived in Dallas, he knew what happened there, what it looked like, what it felt like, even how it smelled. The Twin Cities affiliate needed him to tell *that* story. So at a one-hour fundraising breakfast attended by four hundred people, he helped the audience imagine a place where people living with cancer could receive emotional and social support outside sterile hospital walls:

It felt like I was going into someone's house. Right off the bat, when you walk in—"I'm not in a church basement, it doesn't smell like a hospital, I'm not in a little room with bare walls that's very clinical." I didn't feel like I had to walk in and say, "Hello; my name is Derek Cotton, and I have cancer." It's a totally different feeling. You walk into a Gilda's Club and you're in a home. And after a while, it sort of becomes your second home.

The first time I went, a very cheery woman met me at the door and said, "Hi, how are you? Let's go chat." So we go to this little room and it was like sitting in someone's den. I told her "I don't know why I'm here. I have cancer and I don't know what I'm looking for. I'm just lost."

She said, "We can handle that." And she showed me around.

They had cooking classes to better your diet, art, music, all sorts of different activities every day of the week. Even stuff for my boys: kids' night, games, movies, popcorn. There was a potluck every month. Sometimes, I'd just go there in the afternoon to do my work. I felt comfortable there. It was a place to go where my boys and I were understood, where we felt like regular people. I actually felt like I could get away from my cancer at Gilda's Club.

I was surprised when I moved to Minneapolis and there wasn't a Gilda's Club. The Mayo Clinic is near here, there are major health corporations headquartered here. It's a big city. I just assumed there would be one . . .

Derek's story touched people at the breakfast fundraiser—many of whom knew only too well the emotional and psychological needs of someone dealing with cancer. In that one hour, with Derek's help, the organization raised nearly $500,000 toward its capital campaign. He made a difference for Gilda's Club Twin Cities, which opened its signature red doors in 2014.

As an advocate in one of our workshops recently remarked, "It seems to me that everybody is just one incident away from becoming an advocate for a cause." In Derek's case, that incident was a cancer diagnosis. For Loren, it was the loss of her brother in a distracted driving crash; for Theresa, it was witnessing her son's and other students' allergic reactions; and for Zach, it was a proposed law that disputed the legitimacy of his family. What drives you to be an advocate may likewise be a significant event, a response to what you see happening around you, a whole lifetime of experiences, or a value or belief that dwells at your very core. Whatever that initial impetus is, whether life-altering or quietly significant, it transforms into advocacy when you "answer the call" to make a positive difference for yourself and others, for your community or the world.

What difference did Loren, Theresa, and Zach's advocacy make?

- Loren, an advocate for stricter distracted driving laws, gets e-mails from young people who pledge to stop texting while driving. She says reading the e-mails (for example, one saying, "Thank you so much, you totally changed my mind") keeps her going and enables her to tell the difficult story of her brother's death.

- After hearing Theresa's story, accompanied by a talk from an allergist, parents at the Brooklyn grade school fully cooperated with new school policies regarding allergens packed in school lunches.

- When Zach finished his three-minute address to the Iowa House of Representatives, the crowd erupted in cheers. He didn't know that the speech had been recorded, and it was posted the next day on YouTube. Three days later, it had more than a million hits, was being covered by CNN, ABC, MSNBC, and CBS, and quickly became a powerful prompt for national dialogue—the most-watched political video on YouTube that year.

What keeps you going? What *will* keep you going? Use the following exercise to find out.

EXERCISE

MY SIX-WORD REASON

Objective: *Explain, briefly, how you got here and why you're an advocate.*

Use this exercise to:
- Claim your identity as an advocate, if you're just starting out
- Refocus your story, if you're already speaking as an advocate
- Pinpoint the reason you're telling your story
- Find concise, effective language
- Generate headlines and hooks

How short can a story be? Fredric Brown is credited with the shortest horror story: "The last man on Earth sat alone in a room. There was a knock at the door." Ernest Hemingway supposedly was once dared to write a story in six words. He penned, "For sale: baby shoes, never worn." In 2006, the online storytelling magazine SMITH (www.smithmag.net) asked writers to summarize their lives in six words. The Six-Word Memoir® project spawned a popular book series that includes "terse true tales" of the human experience such as:

Joined Army. Came out. Got booted.—Johan Baumeister
Learning disability, MIT. Never give up.—Joe Keselman

In 2010, journalist Michele Norris began asking her readers to submit their six-word thoughts about race and cultural identity. She's turned it into an online archive called The Race Card Project, (http://theracecardproject.com) with candid contributions such as "I am both, not just one."

My Six-Word Reason is our spin on the Hemingway, SMITH and Race Card challenges. We use this exercise to jumpstart our workshops and focus advocates on their **personal reasons for speaking their stories.**

The Exercise
1. Imagine someone asks you, "*Why* are you an advocate for this cause or organization?"

MY SIX-WORD REASON *(continued)*

2. Write your answer—in just six words. Not five words, not seven. Six.

Here are a few examples:

An art mentor changed my life.
Jamal, a board member for an
organization that pairs artists with
disadvantaged youth

Diagnosed with breast cancer. Still here!
Carol, breast cancer awareness advocate

I've seen too many hungry children.
Roberta, an advocate for ending
world hunger

"I love life, justice and humanity."
—Ocean Robbins

"Son's near death brought new life."
—Theresa Greenleaf

"Gilda's Club gave me a home."
—Derek Cotton

"Love is what makes my family."
—Zach Wahls

Some important guidelines:

- This is a *personal reason*, not a goal. *I've seen too many hungry children,* not *I want to end world hunger. Gilda's Club gave me a home,* not *We should have a Gilda's Club.*
- Think of the personal values that lie at the core of your reason; tap into those.
- Use your six words however you'd like. Your reason may be a full sentence or it may be two three-word phrases.
- Your reason might capture the one moment that drove you to be an advocate, an entire lifetime or a core belief.
- Don't worry about finding *the* right six words. Generate as many reasons as you'd like.
- Give yourself time. Keep track of your work. Save your reasons and return to them later. You'll definitely end up using one or two when you speak.

_____ _____ _____ _____ _____ _____

_____ _____ _____ _____ _____ _____

_____ _____ _____ _____ _____ _____

_____ _____ _____ _____ _____ _____

When Stories Work

Think of a time when you were moved *and* motivated by someone's personal story. Not *just* moved—to laughter, anger, joy, or compassion—but actually motivated to *do* something. You listened to the story and then signed on the dotted line. You made a call or sent a text. You reconsidered your actions, rethought a belief, or repeated the story to someone else. What was it about the story that made you take action?

Chances are it wasn't the story alone that made an impact.

Here's the secret truth that successful advocates and the groups who rely on them know: as much as we may believe absolutely in the power of story to engage and move audiences, advocating well with a personal story is not a call to simply "Insert Story Here." No matter how powerful a story may be, if an advocate is not suitably prepared to tell it, the story will miss the mark. But by paying attention to five distinctive qualities, the well-told advocacy story is within anyone's reach. Before we look at those five qualities, let's consider what might lead to a less than successfully told advocacy story.

> **Advocating well with a personal story is not a call to simply "Insert Story Here."**

Generally, there are two ways of telling an advocacy story that can cause it to fall short: *raw* telling and *canned* telling. When you hear a raw telling, you might perceive the advocate as nervous, fragile, unfocused, or out of control. He or she may ramble on too long or seem overly frank. Often, your response to a raw telling is to feel *for* the advocate, rather than connect *with* the advocate. A canned telling, by comparison, feels overly prepared: it appears slick, detached, scripted. You know a canned telling when you hear one. It's when your first response is, "He's told that story a lot," or even, "She's really good at this." Stories you perceive as either raw or canned distract you from the advocate's purpose and focus you instead on the advocate himself or herself. A raw telling may make you worry about the advocate's emotional state; a canned telling may make you skeptical of the advocate's intent.

While no one intentionally aims to present a story as raw or canned, new advocates often have impulses that can lead— unintentionally, but understandably—to raw or canned tellings. Here are two of those impulses.

Impulse #1: Keeping It Real

New advocates sometimes say, "I don't want to lose the emotion or the freshness of telling my story, so I'll just wing it." While you should always bring genuine emotion and passion to your communication, relying solely on this approach is risky.

Why? Because without preparation, winging it may result in a raw telling—unfocused and unstructured. Speaking off-the-cuff and from the gut may be completely appropriate in other situations, but not when you're working as an advocate. It can place you in an emotionally vulnerable spot, doing disservice to your story and your cause. With media interviews, especially, lack of preparation means you'll be at the reporter's mercy. As you'll see, there are ways to be both genuine *and* prepared when telling your stories.

Impulse #2: Feeding the Fear

Any type of public speaking can be intimidating; sharing a personal story only increases the anxiety, and may cause you to either under-prepare (raw) or over-prepare (canned). You probably know that public speaking is one of humankind's greatest fears, and that most people dread it more than death. Every year, it seems, another public opinion poll supports this attitude. Ask people to name their top fears, and public speaking will rank among the top five. It's clear that putting yourself in the spotlight can be an anxiety-ridden activity—without preparation and practice, that is. People often feel the same about media interviews, fearing that all reporters are either "out to get them" or won't understand the point. Actually, what reporters really want is a good story, told well.

The nervousness people feel going into any public presentation can keep them from adequately preparing and result in their showing up raw. Ironically, nervousness can also lead to a canned presentation or interview.

We once coached a woman preparing to tell her story for the first time. It dealt, tragically, with the loss of two of her family members in two separate drunk driving crashes. In preparing for a coaching session, she e-mailed us a script, saying, "This is what I plan to read." We noted immediately that she had written her story in the third person:

Fears through the Years

A recent survey of Top Five Fears places public speaking alongside "identity theft" and "mass shootings." In the 1980s, it competed with "nuclear destruction." In the 1970s, "shark attack."[4]

"When she was 12, her mother died in a car crash and the little girl couldn't understand how this could happen." In the final sentence, she revealed, "I was that little girl."

While this may have been a dramatic approach to her story, our conversations revealed the real reason she had written it this way: She was terrified of being unable to control her emotions in the act of telling. By removing herself from the story and reading it word for word, she was protecting herself emotionally. The result, however, might have come across as a recited, canned, even gimmicky telling.

After some coaching, the woman decided to tell her first-person story; and she gave a more heartfelt, if somewhat less polished, telling. There are ways to be both confident *and* extemporaneous when telling your stories. (This advocate's initial impulse to protect herself emotionally is also an example of the type of personal negotiations you may make as you prepare to move "from private to public." For a discussion of this important aspect of the process, see Chapter 11, Moving from Silence to Story.)

Striking the Balance

Between the raw and canned extremes, you'll find the perfect balance for sharing your personal stories as an advocate: neither under- nor over-prepared, neither fragile nor distanced, media-ready, and not at a reporter's mercy. The well-told advocacy story is both crafted and flexible, and the well-prepared advocate is both authentic and focused on the message—not just moving audiences, but motivating them to act.

THE RAW STORY	THE WELL-TOLD ADVOCACY STORY	THE CANNED STORY
Under-prepared	Practiced	Over-rehearsed
Emotionally fragile	Emotionally engaging	Emotionally distanced
Unstructured	Crafted	Slick, polished
Nervous	Present	Detached
Impromptu	Improvisational	Scripted
Unfocused	Flexible	Rigid
No apparent messages	Clear link to messages	Messages sound contrived
Vulnerable	Authentic	Distanced
At the mercy of the media	Media-ready	Sensationalized
Focused on advocate	Focused on audience	Focused on effect
Unrestrained	Genuine	Insincere
Audience feels bad for speaker	Audience connects with speaker	Audience analyzes speaker

Five Qualities of the Well-Told Advocacy Story

To strike the right balance between raw and canned tellings, bear these five qualities in mind each time you prepare to advocate with a personal story. These are the hallmarks of a well-told advocacy story. We'll explore these qualities throughout *Living Proof*, but here's a quick introduction.

1. Advocacy Stories are Focused. Telling a personal story to a loved one late at night differs from sharing it with a therapist, which differs from telling it at a party. In each situation, the reason for telling your story changes, and while you may not always think about *why* you tell your stories, there *is* intent. Telling your personal story as an advocate demands that you be explicit in your intent. The more tightly you link your stories to your goals and messages, the more successful your advocacy.

> "I was advocating for parents of kids with severe allergies. I was also advocating for my son, Jack. I needed other parents to know that the safety of all children is of paramount importance, that their cooperation is necessary and appreciated."
> **Theresa Greenleaf, about speaking to other school parents about awareness of food allergies**

2. Advocacy Stories Point to the Positive. Every story, at its core, is about change. The change may be large or small, dramatic or subtle, a seismic upheaval or a slight shift. It may be a personal change or a change you see around you. But there *is* a change. And when you speak as an advocate, the change in your story always points to a positive future.

> "How do I tell my story in a way that leaves the listener hearing a positive message of triumph rather than a story of victimization? I do not want to be seen as a victim or have people feel sorry for me. I want them to see people have value."
>
> **Becky Blanton, advocate for the homeless**

3. Advocacy Stories are Crafted. While all of us are born storytellers, we may not all be *practiced* storytellers. Sharing your personal story as an advocate requires you to explore and practice some fundamentals of storytelling. Those fundamentals include arranging and revising, choosing and polishing language, and editing—one of the most useful skills you can develop as you prepare your stories, especially for media interviews.

> "People love when I mention the ice cream cone-shaped swimming pool my dad grew up with; how he learned that 'blood is thicker than ice cream.' Once you find a good phrase that makes people smile, keep it."
>
> **Ocean Robbins, peace and environmental advocate, grandson of Baskin-Robbins ice cream company founder**

4. **Advocacy Stories are Framed.** For your story to stand as compelling living proof, it cannot stand alone. It must be framed, indicating the particular way you'd like audiences to view or understand it and its importance—you must tell people what your story is, and what it is not. Framing can mean the difference between a story that's perceived as heartfelt and genuine, and one that's seen as whining, self-serving, or preachy. Framing refers to the things you say that help your audience receive your story—and you—as intended.

> "It is not a plea for sympathy. It's about what we can learn from this."
> **Loren Vaillancourt, on telling the story of losing her brother in a traffic accident involving a distracted driver**

5. **Advocacy Stories are Practiced.** Somewhere between raw telling and canned telling is the style of speaking that's effective in most situations. It features your natural speaking style, it's genuine, and it's confident. We call it "improvisational speaking," and it requires practice.

> "I practice. I practice and practice *ad nauseam*. And the story will change a little bit and the messages will change a little bit—but I've learned to go with the flow."
> **Kathy Kastan, heart health advocate**

Qualities of a Well-Told Advocacy Story

 **Focused**

 **Pointed to the Positive**

 **Crafted**

Framed

Practiced

Chapter 2

Map Your Experience

Explore the Entire Landscape

Becky Blanton is a journalist who, at times, has been homeless. The last time was following the death of her father, when she spent 18 months living in a 1975 Chevy van parked at a Walmart. In telling the story, she says:

> Life itself assigns us our causes.[1]
> —**Mary Pipher**

> I don't know when or how it happened, but the speed at which I went from being a talented writer and journalist to being a homeless woman, living in a van, took my breath away. I hadn't changed. My I.Q. hadn't dropped. My talent, my integrity, my values, everything about me remained the same. But I had changed somehow. I spiraled deeper and deeper into a depression.[2]

Then a friend found Becky and told her that an essay she wrote about her father a year before had been selected for the book *Wisdom of Our Fathers: Lessons and Letters from Daughters and Sons*.[3] The editor was the late Tim Russert, then host of NBC's *Meet the Press*. On tour to promote the book, Russert talked enthusiastically about Becky's essay. The irony of this—that her work was being noted in the national media while she lived in a parked van—struck Becky deeply and marked the beginning of her emotional recovery, her return to work, and the eventual end of her homelessness.

Of course, there's more to the story than that. There were the periods of couch-surfing, caring for her cat and Rottweiler, dealing with summer heat and winter cold—and what Becky learned about societal attitudes toward the homeless.

A year later, Becky was given a six-minute opportunity to tell her story publicly for the first time. She needed to decide what—of this deeply personal and complex experience—would be best to tell for the benefit of others.

It took a week of wrestling with the story to come up with the speech I did. I lay in the back of the van (I still drive it) and put myself back in time to relive parts of the experience. I had to drill down to the raw emotions of the experience and convey in six minutes what I'd learned and experienced in eighteen months. I asked friends who had recently learned of my situation what they wanted to know. I took that into account.

When you ask someone, "Will you tell me your story?" what have you really asked? Are you asking them to begin from their earliest memory, walk you briskly through the awkward teen years, detail their adult milestones, then describe the eggs they had for breakfast, say how their day's been, and end with whatever thoughts they had circling just before you asked them to tell you their story?

Probably not. Few people have that kind of recall, and few listeners have that kind of patience. But when you are first asked to tell your story as an advocate, or when you first consider sharing your story, the landscape can seem just as vast: Where do I begin? How much do I tell? What *is* my story?

Don't be paralyzed by thinking you must find the *right* story, the *one* story you'll tell whenever you speak or give an interview. None of us has just one story to tell. And as we'll see in later chapters, *what* you tell as an effective advocate always will be determined by the context: by the goals of your advocacy, the audiences you want to affect, and the key messages you want to convey. Each time you tell your stories, you'll select bits of your experience and arrange them differently for impact with that particular context. That's the "focus" required of a well-told advocacy story.

> **Before you get focused, give yourself time for some free, unfettered exploration.**

But before you get focused, give yourself time for some free, unfettered exploration. An important first step in deciding *what to tell* is to pull back and consider *what happened*—to explore everything you have in your experience that is potential story material.

The process of reflecting on experience, of catching the fragments of life that have fallen through the cracks of memory, is ongoing and different for everyone. Master storyteller Jack Maguire, borrowing a phrase from Walt Whitman's poem, "Song of Myself," calls the process "loafing and inviting the soul." It requires us to slow down and be mindful, to "restimulate the kinds of personal memories that make for good stories to tell."[4] It's particularly important for you, as an advocate, to take this time to reflect—because in the process you may find that the story you *thought* you would tell is not the one you end up telling. Or, at least, it's not the only one.

For most advocates, there is a "core narrative," a story that revolves around an important event or events. That core narrative may have jumped immediately to mind when you considered your Six-Word Reason, and it may be the very impetus for your advocacy. But even if you have a good idea of what your core narrative is, stay open to other parts of your experience that you may not yet

> **As you reflect on your experience, do so without judgment. Enjoy this free, private exploration of what should be made public.**

consider important to share. As you reflect on your experience, do so without judgment. Enjoy this free, private exploration of what should be made public. Author Shirley Jackson, writing in *Experience and Fiction* (1968), suggests a way to approach life to find its stories: "attack it in the beginning the way a puppy attacks an old shoe. Shake it, snarl at it, sneak up on it from various angles."[5]

Use the following exercise, the Story Map, to shake and snarl at the whole of your experience: everything you've seen, heard, said, and felt that urged you to speak out. Obviously, no one can access and recount all those experiences, and you won't bring everything you remember with you each time you speak.

> "Inevitably, familiar memories will take on surprising new life, buried memories will resurface, and you will find yourself instinctively weaving all these memories together with story threads."[6]
> **—Jack Maguire, author and storyteller**

Not everything will be relevant or safe or appropriate to disclose. But this is where public advocacy begins: in private reflection.

STORY MAP

Objective: *Create a visual map of your experience.*

Use this exercise to:
- Explore the landscape of your experience
- Recall the details of your experience
- Find the potential for vivid and engaging living proof
- Create a visual reference you can return to again and again
- Look for stories and moments you may have overlooked

For this exercise, you'll construct a visual map of the experiences that led you to be an advocate. If that sounds like a huge investment of time or if you don't consider yourself a gifted visual artist, try not to worry about it. You can give as little or as much time to this as you'd like: sketch it out quickly or make it the basis of an elaborate and ongoing journal of your experience. Either way, it's important to find out what you've got to work with. Story Map asks you to be expansive, to generate as much material as you can, much more than you could possibly use—a life story so big and full of detail that you'd never be able to tell it in one sitting.

The Exercise

1. **Use whatever media is comfortable and at hand.** Use a pencil and paper, a pen and the back of a napkin, a marker and whiteboard, sticky notes on the wall, or an app on your computer or tablet. Have your note-taking method with you to record ideas, thoughts, emotions, and attitudes that come up while creating the Story Map.

2. **Draw an elongated oval.** Imagine you've drawn it around the whole bundle of experiences that made you want to speak out. Within this oval there may be a lifetime of events or perhaps only a period of your life.

3. **Draw a horizontal line** through the center of your oval, with the ends of the line extending beyond the oval.

STORY MAP *(continued)*

4. **Label the area to the left of the oval *Then* and the area to the right *Now*.** *Then* represents you before your journey to become an advocate. *Now* is you as an advocate. The line connecting them is your timeline of events: this happened, then this happened, then this.

5. **Mark and label events and moments on the timeline with X's or dots.** Begin with the obvious elements of your core narrative: key incidents or events. But don't forget the small moments. At this point, nothing is unimportant. Get it all in there. This is your private exploration.

6. **Populate your map.** Stories are about people. Who was with you at various points in this experience? Who did you see or speak to? Who was watching you? Who left you a voicemail or sent you a text? Locate and label those people with X's or dots.

That's the basic structure of the Story Map—the universe of your experience, the moments that occurred, and the people involved (the setting, the plot, and the characters).

The Story Map is, of course, only one tool for reflecting on your lived experience. If you're a writer, a journal-keeper, or an artist or have worked with a therapist, counselor, or spiritual leader, you've no doubt found other ways to explore life's landscape. Still, give the Story Map a try; advocates find it a useful tool for capturing elements of experience in visual form and building a solid foundation for future work.

Some Guidelines

- It's up to you how detailed and elaborate you make your map.
- As you fill in the map, it may help to pull out a photo album or two, or look back at a calendar.
- Talk to the friends, family members, colleagues, and others who shared your experiences.
- Take note of sensory memories that return as you're reflecting on your experience—what you saw, felt, heard, or smelled. You'll want to evoke some of those senses when telling your story. See the exercise called Making Language Live, page 97.
- You'll return to the map a number of times, so make multiple copies.

Chapter 3

Focus Your Stories

IN THIS CHAPTER:

❏ Choosing what to tell

❏ Clarifying your goals, your audiences, and your key messages

Choose What to Tell

Finding your advocacy stories begins with trying to remember how things happened. You plot out your experience (using the Story Map or another memory aid) to recall episodes, events, and details. But telling stories is not just reciting life events as they occurred. It's the selecting of moments, and arranging them in creative ways, that make a story. Before doing that, all we have is experience.

> "When an experience takes root in our lives, it often grows up into a story".[1]
> —**John Elder,**
> **writer and environmentalist**

> "All memories are not stories. Cooking up egg foo yung is not a story".[2]
> —**Roger Schank,**
> **director, Institute for**
> **Learning Sciences,**
> **Northwestern University**

To find the stories among your experiences, you have to decide which parts to select and arrange. "The ability to find story in your life depends upon cutting it into pieces, and the nature of the stories you find depends on how you slice them," writes autobiographer Tristine Rainer in *The Story of Your Life.*[3] Take another look at the Story Map you created in the previous chapter. Imagine literally slicing it up by drawing vertical lines at various points.

There are countless ways you might do this, taking a moment from here, an image from there, an insight from one day and a snippet of conversation from another. You might cut a wide swath

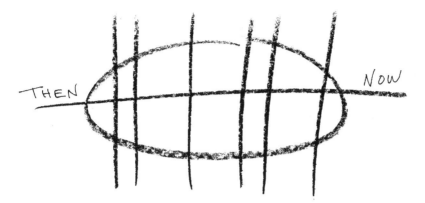

from the center or thin slivers from either end. But you can't tell your whole experience. So how do you choose?

On one level, the choices you make about what to tell are determined by how you feel generally about "going public" with your personal experience. Decisions about personal disclosure are different for everyone, and as you move into the space between the private and the public realms, you may encounter challenging issues and valuable personal insights. We address aspects of this part of the process—managing emotions, addressing self-censorship, considering matters of safety—in Chapter 11, Moving from Silence to Story.

Regardless of how you navigate the space between the private and the public, however, your choices about what to tell always should be guided by your advocacy goals, your audiences, and the messages you hope to convey. In this way, your advocacy stories become focused.

Focus on Your Goals and Your Audience

Whenever you tell a personal story, you tell it for a reason. You may share a story with a loved one to explain yourself or to become closer. You may tell your story to a therapist to make sense of a behavior or to heal. You may tell stories at parties to entertain or commiserate with friends. When you tell your story as an advocate, you do so to make a difference. And the clearer you can be about what that difference is, the more focused and successful your story will be.

> **When you tell your story as an advocate, you do so to make a difference. The clearer you can be about what that difference is, the more focused and successful your story will be.**

Before trying to answer, "*What* is my story?" ask "*What am I trying to do* with my story?" Knowing your goals makes it easier to choose what to tell, what not to tell, and focus your story. It also gives *you* focus. The reason for sharing your story needs to be clear to you—so you can make it clear to your audience.

You have both general and specific goals to reach with your story. *General goals* are long-term end results of your advocacy. General goals describe the better world you imagine, the difference you ultimately want to make: "To create a healthier planet" or "To change attitudes about homelessness." You won't reach a general goal with one speech, one interview, or one story. But you can definitely be of some help in getting there.

Specific goals, on the other hand, are what you hope to achieve at the time you speak: "To move the people at this fundraiser to fill out their donation cards" or "To get people to march with us" or "To have listeners call their doctors to discuss their risk factors." It's important to be clear about your specific goals so you can be realistic about what you want to achieve each time you tell your story.

If you are working with an advocacy organization or group, the group likely has specific goals that are part of their long-term advocacy strategy or a particular campaign or initiative. Be sure you know what the group's goals are and how they line up with your personal goals.

Just as well-told advocacy stories are focused on goals, both general and specific, they are focused on audiences, both general and specific. Your *general audiences* are those broadly defined groups of people you hope to reach. You probably had a general audience in mind when you first decided to go public: "People who also care about protecting the environment" or "Other students." Your *specific audiences* are the actual, living, breathing people you

> "Be very, very, very clear about your motives and your goals. When you know what you want to do with your story you'll know if you've achieved it. I want people who hear my story to reconsider what it means to be homeless. I want my story to spark conversations. I want it to change the way people see each other and themselves. I want it to inspire people. I want to make people feel like they aren't the only ones going through tough times— because they aren't."
>
> **—Becky Blanton, advocate for the homeless**

To get a complete picture of the specific audience for your next talk or interview, see "Being Audience-Centered" (in Chapter 7, p. 126) and "Know Your Target Audience" (in Chapter 8, p. 153).

speak to: the crowd who hears you at a rally or the commuters who listen to your radio interview.

When you know your audience, you know better what stories to tell and how to tell them. Of course, the degree to which you can know an audience will vary with each speaking or interview situation. In some cases, you will have a close knowledge of your audience, as when you're speaking to family or community members. In those instances, you may know what your audience values and how they think. In other cases, as when you're interviewed for print or broadcast media, you may have only general information about the readership or viewership and will need to construct a composite based on what you know about values or interests. In either case, it's fair to say that you can never know *too* much about your audience. Chapters 8 and 9, as well as the Prep Sheets in Chapters 13 and 14 of *Living Proof*, provide questions to consider as you assemble a complete picture of the specific audience for your next talk or interview.

Why is it so critical to consider your audience and goals when telling your story as an advocate? Because advocacy is a persuasive act. When you speak, you are asking others to *do something* as a result of hearing your experience. Focusing on your goals and your audience helps you know what the *something* is you're asking of your audience.

The illustration below shows a range of persuasive goals you may set when you tell your story as an advocate, from having your audience gain a basic awareness of an issue to having them take specific actions such as lending financial support or attending an event. It is helpful, each time you tell your story as an advocate, to consider where on this spectrum you sit. It's also helpful, when working with an organization or group, to understand how your story fits within the goals of the larger campaign, movement, or strategy. In Chapter 7, we look at what your audience's attitude toward your persuasive goal or goals might mean for how you present your story—see "Being Audience-Centered" (page 126)—and we look more closely at persuasive speaking and social movement strategies in Chapter 12, Public Speech, Public Narrative (page 205).

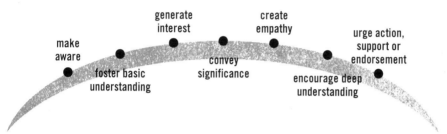

Use the following two exercises to explore how understanding your goals and audiences can help you focus and shape your story.

EXERCISE

IDENTIFY YOUR GOALS AND AUDIENCES

Objective: Be specific about what you want to achieve and whom you hope to reach.

Use this exercise to:
- Focus, focus, focus

The Exercise
- Fill the chart below with general and specific audiences and goals. How completely you are able to fill out the chart will depend upon where you are currently in your planning and preparation. If you have an upcoming talk or interview scheduled, you may have a clear sense of who your specific audience will be (see Chapters 7 and 8, Deliver Powerful Presentations and Give Great Interviews). Or, at this point in your process, you may only be able to name your general audiences. If that's the case, imagine some potential specific audiences as you explore this exercise.

  In this exercise and the next, we use the examples of Loren Vaillancourt (advocate for safe driving) and Kathy Kastan (advocate for women's heart health).

GENERAL AUDIENCES Broadly defined groups I hope to reach	GENERAL GOAL My long-term result	SPECIFIC AUDIENCES Actual persons at my event or interview	SPECIFIC GOAL What I hope to achieve when I speak
Teenagers, Parents	Reduced incidence of distracted driving crashes and deaths	Teens at this high school assembly	To have them reflect, consider and change their behavior.
Women, Legislators, Doctors	Reduced rates of heart disease in women	Women in the audience at this conference	To have them understand the importance of paying attention to their bodies.

IDENTIFY YOUR GOALS AND AUDIENCES *(continued)*

GENERAL AUDIENCES Broadly defined groups I hope to reach	GENERAL GOAL My long-term result	SPECIFIC AUDIENCES Actual persons at my event or interview	SPECIFIC GOAL What I hope to achieve when I speak

LINK TO YOUR GOALS AND AUDIENCE

Objective: Let your specific goals and audiences shape your story.

Use this exercise to:
- Find bits of experience to shape into focused stories

The Exercise
1. **List your specific audience** in the left-hand column of the table provided here.
2. **List a specific goal** in the center column of the chart. This may be your personal goal or the goal of the organization you represent.
3. **Return to your Story Map** and use it to help fill in the right-hand column. For each audience and goal you've listed, look for the moments in your Story Map that demonstrate the importance of that goal.

My Specific Audience	My Specific Goal	Moments That Show Why The Goal Is Important
Teens at this high school assembly	*To have them reflect, consider and change their behavior.*	*The morning I woke up and realized I had become an only child because of someone else's actions.*
Women in the audience at this conference	*To have them understand the importance of paying attention to their bodies.*	*The times when I had not paid attention to my own symptoms for 8 months.*

LINK TO YOUR GOALS AND AUDIENCES *(continued)*

My Specific Audience	My Specific Goal	Moments That Show Why The Goal Is Important

Focus on Key Messages

Heart health advocate Kathy Kastan went from being an "eager but anxious" first-time speaker to a national spokeswoman. The main advice she now gives to other advocates is on the mark:

> Your story is important, yes. Your story is significant, yes. But the most important thing, if you want to make a difference, is to focus on why it's important to the people you're talking to. Get to those key messages.

Key messages say what you want your audience to act upon or learn. Key messages help decide what story you tell and what parts you emphasize. For presentations or talks, key messages determine how you structure your content. For media interviews, they're the main points you'll cover, regardless of how an interview proceeds. Just as well-told advocacy stories are focused on goals and audiences, they are focused on key messages.

How do you know what messages are key messages? Think: "If nothing else, I want my audience to know, understand and do *this* after hearing my story." Key messages are the minimal requirements for what you communicate. You want audience members to repeat your key messages to others. You want journalists and reporters to highlight those messages in their stories. Strong key messages form the backbone of your presentation or media interview, and ensure that your advocacy engages both "the heart and the head."

Here are some guidelines for composing good key messages.

- **Key messages are full sentences**. "Our streets should be safe for our children" is a good key message. "Safety" is not a key message, it's a bullet point.

- **Key messages are statements**. "The first step is to contact our congresspersons" is a good key message. "What's our first step?" is not a key message, it's a question.

- **Key messages are concise and specific.** "Water is everything" is a crisp, clear key message. A paragraph outlining the social and political importance of clean drinking water is not a key message, it's a treatise.

  > Scott Harrison, founder of charity: water, uses the key message "Water is everything" to focus his stories on the organization's mission: bringing clean and safe drinking water to people in developing nations.

- **Key messages are memorable.** "Music can literally make your soul *pop* and move your spirit to a higher and better place," is a key message people will remember. "Empowering young people to affect global change beginning in their local communities by utilizing holistic development and

  > When Glenton Davis, founder of Soul Pop University, used this key message ("Music can literally make your soul *pop*.") in a media interview for *Trends* newspaper, he practically handed the writer the headline: "Nonprofit Organization Makes Music 'Pop' for Students."

  pre-professional programs in creative entrepreneurship" is a mission statement.

- **Key messages should be limited to three points.** If you try to cover seven important messages in a presentation, the audience will have trouble remembering and prioritizing them. In a media interview, it's doubtful you'll have time to hit all seven. Even if you do, some may be edited out.

If you serve as an advocate for a particular organization, you may have key messages handed to you that are critical to the larger advocacy strategy, movement, or campaign. Check with the group's strategists to understand how their key messages may relate to and help shape what you tell.

Because key messages are important to so many aspects of your advocacy success—focusing your story, structuring your presentation, keeping an interview on track—you should have them with you at all times. Post them in your workspace. Carry them in your wallet. Refer to them often as a way of staying focused and on message.

Use the next exercises to write memorable key messages and link them to your story.

EXERCISE

COMPOSE KEY MESSAGES

Objective: Write three key messages that are to the point and memorable.

Use this exercise to:
- Be clear in your intent and message
- Craft language

You'll find that the time spent polishing rough ideas into concise and memorable key messages is well worth it. The clearer your key messages are to you, the clearer they'll be to your audience.

COMPOSE KEY MESSAGES *(continued)*

The Exercise
- **Craft three key messages** that meet the criteria. Think: "If nothing else, this is what I want my audience to understand or do."

Key Message #1

_____

_____

Is it a full sentence?
Is it a statement?
Is it concise and specific?
Is it memorable?

Key Message #2

_____

_____

Is it a full sentence?
Is it a statement?
Is it concise and specific?
Is it memorable?

Key Message #3

_____

_____

Is it a full sentence?
Is it a statement?
Is it concise and specific?
Is it memorable?

LINK TO KEY MESSAGES

Objective: *Let your story stand as living proof of your key messages.*

Use this exercise to:
- Focus your story on your key messages
- Find parts of your story that are the strongest for your advocacy goals
- See how different key messages can change your story

How you tell your story and what you tell may change depending on your messages. Use this exercise to determine which parts of your story best support and illustrate your key messages.

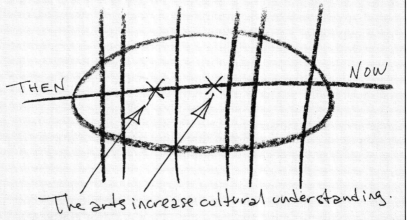

THEN   NOW

The arts increase cultural understanding.

The Exercise

1. **Return to your Story Map.**

2. **Write a key message below your map.** This could be one of the messages you wrote in the previous exercise or it could be a message provided by your sponsoring organization or group.

Use this with the exercise on page 88, *Look Here*, to practice articulating the links between your story and key messages.

LINK TO KEY MESSAGES *(continued)*

2. Draw lines that connect your message to specific moments in your Story Map. Ask:

What moments from my story connect most powerfully to that message?

What moments provide the best example of this message or demonstrate its importance?

3. Repeat this exercise with your key messages each time you prepare for a speech or media appearance. Key messages change; your story will too.

Chapter 4

Point to the Positive

IN THIS CHAPTER:

❏ Naming the positive changes in your stories

❏ Double-checking your readiness to speak out

❏ Steering an interview in the right direction

Stories Are about Change

In its simplest form, a story is a series of events happening to someone, somewhere. Stories are about action, about movement, about what happens to someone as she or he moves from point A to point B to point C. Typically, we refer to this as a story's plot; think of it more simply as the *change* that occurs. When you tell your story as an advocate, the change that is at the heart of your story is always a positive one.

> **When you tell your story as an advocate, the change that is at the heart of your story is always a positive one.**

Does this mean that when you tell your stories, you focus only on the good and the happy or even sanitize your experiences? Far from it. You may have endured great hardship, seen injustices, or suffered great loss. Or you may have enjoyed great successes, been inspired by others, or garnered win after win. Audiences need to hear the true progression of your journey, as you experienced it. But no matter what course your story follows, remember that your primary reason for sharing it is to make a difference. To do so, you must tell your advocacy story in a way that points to the positive — *the positive change in you* and/or *the positive change you want to see*.

Beginning in her late adolescence, Gayathri Ramprasad began to experience bouts of extreme anxiety and depression: "I could hardly eat, sleep or think straight. The only thing I could do was cry."[1] At the time, Gayathri was still living at home in Bangalore, India, in a traditional culture that had no concept of depression as an illness. Her parents insisted her agitation was all in her head. The story she tells now as an advocate for mental health traces her thirty-year dual battle with depression and the associated stigma that constantly "tightened its noose around my neck." As her story follows Gayathri into marriage, a move to the United States, and motherhood, there are many painful moments, such as when her husband discovers her in the backyard "clawing the earth furiously with my bare hands, intent on digging a grave so that I could bury myself alive." Eventually, she is hospitalized and confined in the seclusion room of a psychiatric ward several times a week where she often felt "like a convict on death row."

But Gayathri doesn't end her story there. If she did, she would move us only from point A to point B.

The Positive Change in You

On the Story Map (page 42), you drew an oval and then filled it with the whole of experience that led you to speak out. Bracketing the oval are two words: *Then* and *Now*. Your Story Map shows one way your story is inherently positive: in the *Now*, you have decided to speak out and make a difference. The very fact that you have found the motivation to be an advocate with your stories is evidence of positive change.

But there may be other positive changes that occurred for you between *Then* and *Now*. Those changes may be huge and obvious transformations, or they may be small and subtle shifts:

From adversity to triumph: I was broken, now I am stronger.

From one perspective to another: I used to think that, now I think this.

From ignorance to insight: I was blind, now I see.

You might express the change as one of metamorphosis: "I was A, then B happened; now I've become C." The change can be psychological, physical, literal, or metaphorical.

Here are some examples:

Then: Neither Kathy Kastan nor her physicians recognized the early signs of heart disease. She was ill and ill-informed.

Now: She is an authority on heart-healthy living and a national advocate for raising awareness of heart disease in women.

Changes: From innocence to knowledge. From illness to health. From passivity to action.

Then: Scott Harrison was a New York nightclub promoter living a fast, selfish, and arrogant life, "...chasing models and bottles."

Now: Founder of charity: water, he's dedicating his life to serving others, helping millions get access to clean drinking water.

Changes: From self-interest to compassion. From excess to access.

> "My family story represents a journey from success defined as a life of unlimited consumption, to success defined as a life of unlimited compassion. It is the journey from the old American dream of business accomplishment to a deeper American dream of health and contribution."
> —**Ocean Robbins, peace and environmental advocate**

Then: Loren Vaillancourt was devastated by her brother's death in a car crash.

Now: She's seen how telling her story can make people stop talking and texting while driving.

Changes: From grief to hope. From mourning to motivation.

For Gayathri, a defining moment came when she was a patient in the psychiatric ward, placed again in the seclusion room. Just before closing the door to the room, a nurse offered Gayathri words of compassion and strength that somehow triggered an awakening in her. In the night, she had a startling moment of clarity in which she promised to "fight to restore my dignity," but also to bring hope to the lives of others. Gayathri looks to that moment as the start of her dedication to advocacy.

Then: Gayathri Ramprasad was paralyzed by depression and the terror of speaking out.

Now: She's a dedicated, vocal advocate for mental health and founder of ASHA International.

Changes: From inward turmoil to outward action. From seclusion to connection.

Your change—the "something that happens to someone, somewhere"—is what turns experience into story. The audience will be listening for it. But if the change you convey is negative, your audience may feel only compassion or pity, or might dismiss your story as "just" confession, complaint, or vent. So it's important that you can name the positive change that has occurred in you—whether or not you state it explicitly when telling your story. Naming the positive change will help you

> "The stories that stick with me are the stories that have that a-ha moment where something prompts a farmer to make a change. I like the stories of farmers and families who are doing things the conventional way, and then something really prompts them to forge a new path."
>
> **—Drake Larsen, Practical Farmers of Iowa**

> "A big part of how I tell my story of domestic violence is about post-traumatic growth. I'm now more connected to my kids, I'm more authentic, I'm more willing to have an open, honest and direct conversation with someone and not be afraid to do that. I am more grateful for each day. All of these things came out of going through this horrendous experience."
>
> **—Kristin Brumm, domestic violence awareness advocate**

- Decide which parts of your experience to share to communicate that change
- Stay focused on your advocacy goals
- Keep media interviews on track
- Frame your story
- Cast yourself in your story the way you want your audience to see you

Naming your positive change also helps you double-check how ready you are to go public. If you find it difficult to name the positive change and are locked in anger, frustration, grief, or pain, take time to think through your stance as an advocate and how you feel about it. If you can't name your positive change, you may be setting yourself up to tell a raw story: emotionally fragile, vulnerable, at the mercy of the media.

"HIV is not something I expected to happen to me. But fate never puts you in a situation you're not supposed to be in. And HIV gave me some direction in my life. Before HIV, I had an idea of what I wanted to do: I knew I wanted to help people. But I didn't know how I wanted to do that. HIV gave me that purpose. So now I'm giving audiences an example of how young people can overcome adversity every single day, especially LGBT young people."
—Lawrence Stallworth II, HIV/AIDS awareness advocate

The Positive Change You Want to See

The second way in which well-told advocacy stories point to the positive is by giving audiences a clear sense of "the better world" you're advocating for and the true difference you hope your story will make. Whether you mention that better world only briefly ("I'm here today to help ensure this doesn't happen again") or fully describe it ("Here's what we can look forward to if we get this law on the books. First..."), including it in your advocacy is critical. For example, mental health advocate Gayathri Ramprasad speaks of a world "where every man, woman and child suffering from mental illness is provided the love and support they need to thrive in life." By pointing clearly to the change you want to see, you

- Invite the audience to envision themselves as part of the positive change
- Help the audience make the connection between your specific life experiences and the issue or action that affects them or others
- Remind audiences that with your storytelling, you are ultimately asking something of them: to be more aware, change a behavior, adopt a new plan of action, or write a check that will help create change. Unless you point to the positive, better world, telling your story does not give your audience tangible reasons to care, reflect, or invest.

Here's an example of what happens when an advocacy story doesn't point to the positive. It's a transcript of a local television news broadcast—with names changed—in which an advocate inadvertently plays into the negative attitude set by reporters.

The news feature is about an upcoming 3K Run/Walk to raise money for lung cancer research. An in-studio news anchor introduces the story, then hands it off to a reporter conducting a live interview with a man who recently lost his wife to lung cancer. She left behind three children. This was not only devastating, but shocking to them because the woman had never smoked a day in her life (smoking causes most lung cancers, but causes of other lung cancers are unknown).

While the man is obviously committed to his cause, it's clear from his attitude that he's still distraught, having lost his wife only months ago. He manages to deliver some key messages at the end of the interview that point to the positive change he wants to see (such as more awareness of the disease, more funding for research), but it is not enough to deliver hope and motivate us to help. Instead, the reporters' questions focus on the family's loss and feelings of helplessness. You see a grieving man, not an advocate pointing to the positive change he envisions and that will be made possible by the fundraiser.

On location at the local cancer center, the reporter asks the man to "Tell us about your wife." The man tells of the difficulty diagnosing the disease and realizing "there was nothing we could do."

REPORTER: Okay. What did you feel like when you first found out?

MAN: Well, it was a whirlwind of emotions. You really

can't—I probably can't describe adequately what you feel, but, umm, disbelief, shock. You're sitting there enjoying somewhat of a normal family and then all of a sudden your wife— healthy, never smoked a day in her life—is being told she has lung cancer.

REPORTER: Mm-hmm.

MAN: And so that certainly goes against all the stereotypes you hear. But more importantly, when you, you know, get involved in the treatments here and you find out how many people do suffer from that devastating disease and just the sheer numbers. So, it hasn't been a journey of just one, there's a journey of many. But for us, it was just shocking to go through that.

REPORTER: Now, what is your part in the event coming this weekend, the fundraiser?

MAN: Well, she went through a series of aggressive treatments and to say that she was determined is probably an understatement. But even with the best treatments available, there were still— it wasn't enough to beat the battle, so…

REPORTER: Right.

MAN: So, I think, if anything, just to increase the awareness, hopefully empower people to want to be a part of organizations like this, because there's so many unmet needs in this devastating disease and certainly nobody deserves lung cancer. And so, if we can make people more aware of that and they can provide funding, important funding for treatments and resources, that's a wonderful thing.

Before tossing it back to the anchor, the reporter is compelled to mention: "You have three kids. One of them, Eric, is having a

birthday today. Do you want to say happy birthday to him?" The
man bravely manages a smile to the camera and a "happy birthday."

REPORTER TO ANCHOR: So, we're going to wrap things up
from here. But, isn't this a horrible story Diane? It's so scary to
hear this.

ANCHOR: Yeah, I mean it's one of those things where you ask
yourself, "Okay, what can I do to protect myself?" And really
the answer is not very much.

REPORTER: Nothing you can do for it.

ANCHOR: Yeah, which does not sit well with most of us.

Though the anchor closes with a quick mention of the
upcoming Run/Walk, the somber tone has been set and that's
where it stays. How could this advocate have steered the interview
toward his positive message while still honoring the emotional
content of his story? Perhaps his positive change could be
expressed this way:

Then: Stunned and shocked by losing his wife to lung cancer.

Now: Committed to raising research funding and helping
to prevent deaths.

Changes: From devastation to dedication. From paralysis to
power. From hurt to help.

The Positive Change I Want to See: A great turnout at the
fundraising event; money raised for research; fewer
people experiencing what I have.

With his story pointed positively, the interview might have
gone like this (revisions in italics):

REPORTER: What did you feel like when you first found out?

MAN: Well, it was a whirlwind of emotions. You really can't—I probably can't describe adequately what you feel, but, umm, disbelief, shock. *There are a lot of people here at the Cancer Center who've been through that same shock and disbelief. It's horrible. That's why we're so motivated to come together to do something. We don't want others to have to live through this, and with more funding for research, better treatments and resources, we know we can make a difference.*

This is also a great example of how to reframe your story (Chapter 6: Frame It).

REPORTER: You have three kids. One of them, Eric, is having a birthday today. Do you want to say Happy Birthday to him?

MAN: [to camera] Happy Birthday, Eric. [to reporter] *He'll be joining us with a bunch of his friends at this Saturday's 3K Run/Walk. His class is sponsoring their participation . . . he wouldn't miss it.*

Here's another example of how naming the positive change helps. Becky Blanton, advocate for the homeless, first had the opportunity to tell her story at a TED Global Conference, a popular meeting of minds dedicated to "Ideas Worth Spreading." After telling the audience the story of how she found her way out of homelessness, Becky concluded her presentation by naming the change: "Three years ago I was living in a van in a Walmart parking lot. And today I'm speaking at TED. Hope always, always, finds a way."[2]

Use the following exercises to name your change and point your story toward the positive change you hope to see.

EXERCISE

NAME THE POSITIVE CHANGE IN YOU

Objective: *Articulate what happened between Then and Now, ending in this positive act of advocacy.*

Use this exercise to:
- Decide what parts of your experience to emphasize
- Stay focused on your goals
- Keep media interviews on track
- Double-check how ready you are to go public

Earlier in this chapter, we summarized the positive personal changes expressed in stories told by advocates Kathy Kastan, Scott Harrison, Loren Vaillancourt and Gayathri Ramprasad. Using the same format, how would you name the story of your change?

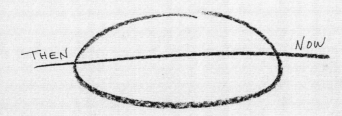

The Exercise

1. **Look at your Story Map** and the words bracketing your experience: *Then* and *Now.* Consider: How are you different now than you were at the start? What do you know now that you didn't know before?

2. **Look again at the examples on page 66,** then fill in the blanks below. Step outside yourself and write it in the third person as someone looking at your story. Use *he* or *she* or refer to yourself by name.

NAME THE POSITIVE CHANGE IN YOU (*continued*)

Write a sentence or phrase that describes you **Then.**		
Write a sentence or phrase that describes you **Now.**		
List words that describe the **change** or **changes**.	**From:**	**To:**
	From:	**To:**
	From:	**To:**
	From:	**To:**
	From:	**To:**

NAME THE POSITIVE CHANGE YOU WANT TO SEE

Objective: Articulate the better world for which you're advocating.

Use this exercise to:
  • Practice describing the goal of your advocacy to others

The Exercise
  1. **Imagine sitting or standing comfortably with an interviewer.** She is intensely interested in your mission and story. Set a timer at 3 minutes, and imagine she asks you these questions:

     What is the change you want to see in the world? What is that better world like?

  2. **Keep talking for the full 3 minutes** and describe as fully as you can what the change is you imagine and what that better world looks like. Use these phrases to begin and return to them if you get stuck:

     I am advocating for . . .
     I am advocating in order to . . .
     What I want to see happen is . . .
     By telling my story I hope . . .

  3. Try this exercise with a partner.

Craft Your Story

The Need to Craft

When we talk about the need to craft personal stories, new advocates sometimes worry that crafting will make their stories feel canned, over-prepared, or slick. But crafting doesn't mean turning your stories into something they're not or pushing them into melodrama. Crafting means applying fundamental storytelling techniques to ensure your audience is engaged.

You are a born storyteller. And you naturally craft your stories, though you may not always be conscious of doing so. Think of a funny story you've told a number of times. Or an episode from your childhood, a brush with

> **Crafting doesn't mean turning your stories into something they're not or pushing them into melodrama.**

greatness, your proudest achievement, or a bad customer service incident you've told frequently. The eighth time you told that story was probably different from the first time. What changed? The first time you told it you may have been remembering it as you went along. When telling it a few more times, you noticed your listeners' attention wandering, so you did some editing. Maybe you found you could hook listeners by starting with the "payoff"—"Did I ever tell you about getting kicked out of my senior prom?" Sometimes you told the story in great detail, other times you summarized it quickly. Often, you did a little of each.

It's this same level of craft you want to apply to your advocacy stories: decide how to assemble the parts of your experience, choose what stays in and what comes out. Adjust the pace to tell your story quickly or in great detail. Use the language of story, which is different from the language used for reporting data. Perform what Robert McKee calls "the creative conversion of life itself into a more powerful, clearer, more meaningful experience."[1]

Assembling the Flexible Story

Being able to scale your story for media sound bites, keynote addresses, and everything in between is one of the most useful skills you can learn as an advocate. Scaling enables you to summarize almost your entire Story Map, as when heart health advocate Kathy Kastan says:

> I went to a doctor feeling strange. He misdiagnosed me, told me I'd be fine. Went jogging in high altitude, collapsed. The symptoms were more serious—came home, saw another doctor. Misdiagnosed again, then found a doctor who got it—but I ultimately needed bypass surgery. Now I'm good. That's my story in a nutshell.

Read more of Kathy's story on page 145.

Former U.S. Representative Tony Coelho, a primary sponsor of the Americans with Disabilities Act, condensed years into just a few phrases when he spoke to fellow legislators and related the incidents leading up to his epilepsy diagnosis:[2]

> Student body president in high school. Student body president in college. I was sought after by different businesses and groups to be involved with their activities and employed by them. I had decided that I wanted to be an attorney. In my

senior year, I changed my mind. I decided I wanted to be a catholic priest. I graduated with honors. I then had a physical exam in order to enter the seminary.

At other times, Coelho added more detail to focus on a particular moment:

I always remember very well what happened and that I walked to the doctor's office from my car, sat in the doctor's office, was told about my epilepsy, got back in my car and drove back to my fraternity house. And I was the same exact person— but only in my own mind. Because the world around me had changed.

> "The first time I told my story was for an edited video piece and I wasn't sure what to say. I thought I had to say everything. 'This happened, then this happened, then this happened.' My descriptions of things were lengthy. The next time, speaking at a fundraiser, I had 7 ½ minutes. At last week's event I had 3 minutes. So one of the things I've learned is that I can be just as effective in three-minutes as I am in seven minutes—and still tell the same story."
>
> —**Derek Cotton, advocate for cancer support services**

You may tell a succinct story to a potential donor while you're sharing an elevator or to the television reporter conducting a short on-camera interview. As a keynote speaker or in a longer interview, you'll have the luxury of more time and can go into more detail. To be ready for any speaking or media situation, your story needs to be flexible, and flexibility comes first from how you assemble your story.

Here's an everyday example.

Let's say you're visiting a friend for the weekend, and you haven't seen each other in a while. To reminisce and catch you up, your friend (apparently highly organized) takes out a stack of five old photo albums. She lays the albums out before you. "This one is all college pictures, this one is vacations…," she says, and gives you a photographic tour of her life. She starts with Album 1, the oldest photos—family milestones like birthday parties and wedding portraits—and together you look at each picture, turning page after page, pausing occasionally to look more closely or to listen as your friend tells what else was happening around a particular moment. You finish Album 1 and move to Album 2 and then 3. At Album 3, she says, "Y'know? We can come back to these vacation shots later if you want to, but they're kind of boring… Florida, Mexico, New York, Florida, Florida…" and she skips to Album 4.

You ask, "Hey, whatever happened to your cousin Byron? He was hilarious…" She reaches for Album 5, and there's the adult Byron mugging for the camera at a barbecue last year. She grabs Album 3 and there's nineteen-year-old Byron on Spring Break, with the same mug. She goes back to Album 1: there's Byron at six years old, sporting a gap-toothed grin. Clearly, Byron is alive and well and as goofy as ever.

It's a simple analogy: assembling your life experiences into stories is like giving someone a photographic tour of your life. Sometimes you show "how it happened." At other times you say, "look here."

Assembling Story 1: How It Happened

Just as your friend began her photo tour with Album 1, you may guide audiences through your story chronologically, pausing at times, sometimes skipping ahead, but keeping things moving forward. You tell *How it Happened*, walking your listeners along the timeline of your Story Map: this happened, then this happened, then this. Album 1, next page, next page. Album 2, next page, next page. This approach is useful when it's important for audiences to understand the order in which things occurred or the effects over time.

When Teresa Opheim shares how the demise of her family's farmstead led to her current role as executive director of Practical Farmers of Iowa, she steps listeners through a chronology of many years:

> I'm a 7th-generation Iowan and I grew up going to my grandparents' farm. After law school I left Iowa, not planning to return. But whenever I came back to visit, I would notice what was happening to my native state. There were fewer and fewer farms and larger and larger fields.... After my grandparents died, their farmstead was sold off and the farmhouse ripped down. About 5 years ago, all that was left were two trees in the ditch. I went by this spring and there are no trees. That's exactly what we don't want to happen in rural Iowa.

Assembling Story 2: Look Here

Another option you might choose is to tell your story the way your friend responded to your question about her cousin Byron—by assembling bits and pieces in random order. This approach gathers scenes into a collage, saying, "Look here. Now here." Chronology isn't important; *Look Here* relies on cumulative effect, so scenes may be out of order. Storyteller Jack Maguire refers to this as the *portrait gallery* approach:[3] Imagine the scenes of your experience framed and hanging on gallery walls or the walls of your home. You shine a flashlight to direct viewers to "Look here. Now here. And now here."

Because chronology isn't important, the *Look Here* approach lets you move backward then forward in time, selecting and narrating the moments you choose. This approach is useful for illustrating specific points, for example, by offering three short scenes that show the importance of one big idea.

Read more of Scott's story on page 146.

When speaking at the Big Omaha tech conference in 2010, Scott Harrison illustrated his key message that "Water is everything" with stories of what he had witnessed in water-deprived villages of Africa. Scott used the *Look Here* organization this way: he told of kids in Northern Uganda who, instead of going to school, walked back and forth along the roads, in the hottest part of the day, carrying 40-pound containers of water on their heads. Then he told of a woman near the border of Sudan, dipping a bucket into a mudhole and saying, "This is the water I take home, like an animal, and give to my kids." Then he described a girl in Ethiopia who, when she gets her period, stops going to school because there are no toilets. Accompanied by Scott's dramatic photographs, his presentation was a literal and vivid gallery of support for his key message: Water is everything.

Adjusting the Pace

Quick. Tell your story in one minute. Now 30 seconds. Now 10 seconds.

No problem, right? Just talk faster, then faster still.

While speed-talking can certainly be an entertaining skill, it's not the most powerful way to engage your audience. The ability to be nimble and to scale your story—without turning it into a tongue-twister—lies in deciding where you spend your storytelling time.

To vary the rate and length of your story, get to know these basic storytelling tools: scene, description, and summary. They're the narrative equivalents of hitting play, pause, and fast-forward on your streaming video or DVD.

Scene. Hit ▶ to tell your story as if it were happening—as when you and your friend looked at individual photos in sequence.

Description . Hit ▐▐ to slow down or freeze your story—as when you and your friend stopped to look at a particular photo and talk about the details and/or when you left the photo and went off on a tangent.

Summary. Hit ▶▶ to zoom through your story—as when your friend condensed her vacations into "Florida, Mexico, New York, Florida, Florida."

Use the following exercise, Right-Size Your Story, to practice assembling your flexible story and adjusting its pace, and the next exercise, What Makes the Cut? to explore some creative ways of organizing events.

EXERCISE

RIGHT-SIZE YOUR STORY

Objective: Practice collapsing and expanding your story

Use this exercise to:
- Learn how to be brief and flexible

This is an exercise with five variations that ask you to assemble your story in different ways and then practice using scene, description, and summary. Keep track of these long and short versions. You'll definitely use them in your advocacy work.

The Exercise
- **Grab your Story Map and a partner.** You could also free-tell and record yourself.

Variation 1: How It Happened
This variation gives you practice summarizing your entire Story Map.
1. Look at your Story Map and give yourself three minutes to summarize the whole thing, from *Then* to *Now*. Tell your story in chronological order, but decide what moments to include.
2. Now give yourself 2 minutes.
3. Now 1 minute.
4. Now 30 seconds.

Variation 2: Look Here
This variation could serve as the basis of an advocacy talk or interview. Remember to clearly state the connection each time you link a scene to a message.

Use this variation with *Link to Key Messages* on page 60.

1. Choose one of your key messages (page 58) .
2. Look at your Story Map and select three scenes that relate to that one message.
3. State the key message, then talk through the scene. Say how they relate.
4. State the message again and talk through the next scene. Say how they relate.
5. State the message again and talk through the next scene. Say how they relate.

RIGHT-SIZE YOUR STORY *(continued)*

Variation 3: Summary
This variation gives you a different way of summarizing moments of your
Story Map.

1. Choose a large section of your timeline, one that covers a good amount of
chronological territory.
2. Summarize that section of time and tell what happened within it.

Variation 4: Description
This variation provides practice fully describing a moment so others can see, hear,
and feel with you.

- Focus on one moment and describe it in as much detail as you can.

Variation 5: Summary-Description-Summary
This variation gives you practice with a very common way of telling your story: by
focusing on some moments, then summarizing others.

1. Select one moment to describe in detail. Look at everything that happens
before that moment and after it.
2. Summarize what happens before, describe the moment in detail, then
summarize what happens after.

EXERCISE

WHAT MAKES THE CUT?

Objective: *Explore creative ways of organizing the moments in your stories.*

Use this exercise to:
- Find bits of experience to shape into stories
- Change the perspective on your experience; step outside yourself to see how versions of your experience may come together differently

Remember that your stories take shape depending on how you slice your experience. And you've got many ways of deciding what makes the cut. If "slicing and cutting" analogies feel too rough for you, there are plenty of others used by filmmakers, writers, folklorists, and artists. What Makes the Cut? is an exercise with five variations that explore these analogies. Each variation asks you to view your experience from a different perspective. Give each one some time; you may find new ways of arranging your experience.

The Exercise
1. Grab your Story Map and some sticky notes. Use the notes to label areas of your map. Or make multiple copies of your map and mark up each one of them.
2. Keep a list of the moments revealed by each of these variations.

Variation 1: Life as a Movie
Think of your Story Map as the raw material for a bio-pic like *Gandhi, What's Love Got to Do With It?* or *Walk The Line.* Just as a screenwriter selects scenes to tell the main character's story (gentle Gandhi, triumphant Tina Turner, determined Johnny Cash), choose elements from your experience to tell your story.

Some labels to apply:
- Great Opening Shot
- The Realization
- Climax of the Story
- My Enemy

- My Hero
- Funny Moments
- Victory Moment
- Great Closing Shot

WHAT MAKES THE CUT? *(continued)*

Variation 2: Life Snapshots

Imagine that you have photos of all the moments in your Story Map. Which would you place into an album of your story?

Some labels to apply:

- Five Best Shots
- The One Shot that Says it All
- My Favorite Shot

Variation 3: The History

Imagine your map is an archaeological timeline like *The Evolution of Dinosaurs* or *A Timeline of Ancient Greece*. How do events on your map fall into periods or eras?

Some labels to apply:

- Geographic Locations
- Time Periods
- Happy Times
- Hard Times

Variation 4: Life's Fabric

The metaphor of fabric arts (stitching, weaving, quilting) is perhaps one of the most common in describing story-making. If you were sewing together your experience into a story, how would you choose the swatches?

Some labels to apply:

- Similar Patterns
- Rough Times
- Smooth Times
- Harmony
- Contrast
- Intricate Weavings

Variation 5: Secret Stash

There may be moments from your Story Map that you'd prefer to keep locked away as not-ready-for-public-presentation. What are the moments on your map that you remove or set aside as you consider going public? (See Chapter 11, Moving from Silence to Story, to reflect on why you might set certain moments aside.)

Some labels to apply:

- Maybe Someday
- If It's Absolutely Necessary
- My Secret

The Language of Lived Experience

Good stories transport listeners to other places and times. They bring to life scenes, characters, and actions. To do this, stories require language that moves beyond the simple reporting of facts to the conjuring of sights and sounds, thoughts and emotions. The language of story is the language of attitude, tone, senses, images, rhythm, and often, poetry.

When LeDerick Horne was in the third grade, he began to realize that his reading level had not kept up with his peers—when he looked at the page, all he saw were groups of letters with no meaning. After a series of tests, he was given the vague diagnosis of having a "neurological impairment." He was separated from his class and placed in the school's resource room—in this case, a teacher's storage closet—then eventually in a special education classroom.

The isolation and separation from his fellow students took a toll on LeDerick socially, and he developed anxiety and self-doubt. Writing was difficult and came slowly. Nevertheless, with the support of family, his own drive, and an increasing desire to fight against a flawed educational system, LeDerick graduated from high school and college. Today he's a powerful advocate for people with disabilities. When he tells his story, he says:

My youth, in central Jersey
has made me worthy of the title

Survivor
Cause I've survived
Yes, I've survived
I didn't "just say no"
I survived
I didn't graduate
I survived
I didn't grow up
I survived…

In addition to being an advocate, LeDerick is a spoken-word poet. A counselor at his two-year college recognized his talent early on and urged him to forget about spelling and grammar… and just write. This license unlocked his creativity. He began using his poetic talent to craft and shape his personal story into a tool of advocacy that now empowers and educates others. "I realized early on that's who I needed to be," LeDerick remembers. "I'm going to be the poet who speaks to folks with disabilities. I'm going to be the poet who talks and represents the folks who have been through special education and have lived that reality. And poetry would be the tool I use to convey my story."

Not everyone has the natural eloquence that LeDerick and other spoken-word poets do (many of them draw on their personal experiences to advocate for others). But you don't need to be a poet, a performer, a writer, or a journalist to tell your story powerfully. You *do*, however, need to elevate your language in ways that will bring your story to life clearly and imaginatively for others. Effective advocates apply the basic craft of expressive language to their storytelling…and expressive language begins in the body.

As an advocate, you bring something to your cause no one else can provide: your lived experience in all its messy humanness. The reason your spoken story differs from a written version in its power to move an audience is that when you speak, your living, breathing body is present. Yours is the body that experienced this story; you are both message and messenger, telling your story as only you know it should be told. And audiences respond to your personal "authorship"—*if* you use language that originates in your lived experience, language that helps audiences understand what things looked, felt, and sounded like to another human body. Writer Mary Pipher describes this power simply: "We all process the world through our bodies. In a profound sense, our bodies are what we have in common."[5]

To bring your story to life for audiences, follow these guidelines:

- **Appeal to all the senses.** Give your audience sensory details to make your story come to life: the look, the feel, the sound, the smell, even the taste of things.

It Starts in the Body

As performer/researcher Tami Spry notes in *Body, Paper, Stage* (2011), the process of reading others' lived experience is a bit like an episode of a television crime drama series:

"It starts with a body, in a place, and in a time. The investigators analyze the body for evidence, the body as evidence, the body of evidence."[4]

Look: *I noticed a fly on the boy's eyelid as he reached out his hand to me.*

Feel: *When I stood in front of the sculpture for the first time, my knees went weak. I was light-headed.*

Sound: *The oil bubbled up, popped, slurped—then nothing.*

Smell: *The forest air smelled like cold mushrooms.*

Taste: *I spoke to the doctor, the taste of the pill still in the back of my throat.*

You don't need to make every moment excessively detailed. That could cause sensory overload. But look for opportunities to get specific when describing moments, objects, and feelings.

- **Tell both outer and inner stories.** You can tell your story from the "outside," saying what happened on the surface: "I got back on the bus and rode home." Or you can go "inside" to tell what you thought and felt: "I got back on the air-conditioned bus, thinking of the face of the child I had just seen. My hands were shaking." Sometimes it's necessary to remain on the outskirts of your story to summarize it quickly. But if you stay outside, you won't give listeners a chance to understand the emotional or sensory content. Conversely, if you stay inside your story, you risk alienating audiences and drawing too much focus to yourself. The most effective storytellers move from outer to inner and back again.

> "It was strange, because at the time—a lot of my friends didn't really know how to deal with me. Y'know: I had cancer. Everyone wants to empathize with you: 'Is there anything I can do?' and all that. When they'd say, 'I understand what you're going through,' I knew what they meant. I used to say the same thing to people. But when you're going through it, you realize, 'You know what? I didn't have a clue before what others were going through.'"
>
> **—Derek Cotton, advocate for cancer support services, spontaneously brings to life the people in his story, their words and his own inner voice**

- **Populate your story.** Stories are about people. While you are the main character (the protagonist), your story involves others. Look for opportunities to describe those populating

95

your Story Map. Quote them. Tell what you said to them and to yourself. Include dialogue.

- **Make creative links.** Use analogies to help your audience make imaginative connections between your story and something else—something familiar to them or something they never would have considered. For example, heart health advocates often say the feeling of a heart attack is "like an elephant stepping on my chest." Remember that analogies and most figures of speech are culturally specific. Consider whether your audience will share the same references you do: for example, Judeo-Christian references like "David vs. Goliath," or whether you're using ethnocentric language (like the American who notes that people from the UK "drive on the *wrong* side of the road").

> "Then, while jogging with my dog one morning, she pulled me into what I thought was just another illegal dump. There were weeds and piles of garbage and other stuff that I won't mention here, but she kept dragging me—and lo and behold, at the end of that lot was the river. I knew that this forgotten little street-end, abandoned like the dog that brought me there, was worth saving. And I knew it would grow to become the proud beginnings of the community-led revitalization of the new South Bronx. And just like my new dog, it was an idea that got bigger than I'd imagined."[6]
>
> **—Majora Carter, sustainable development advocate working to "green the ghetto" of the South Bronx, compares the neglected East River bank to her adopted dog**

Use the following exercise to practice finding creative and expressive language.

EXERCISE

MAKING LANGUAGE LIVE

Objective: Practice drawing creative language from your lived experience.

Use this exercise to:
- Find new ways to express your ideas and story moments
- Remember how you experienced your story
- Create "full-color portraits" for your listeners

Bringing evocative, creative language to personal storytelling takes time: time to remember what the experience was like for you. Time alone, in quiet reflection, then time with a partner to try out your language. Time to look in a thesaurus for just the right word.

This exercise has four variations.

The Exercise
- **Grab your Story Map and a partner.** You could also free-tell and record yourself.

Variation 1: Activating the Senses
1. Choose a moment on your Story Map. Close your eyes and imagine being there: What do you see? Hear? Smell? Is there a particular taste in your mouth? What does your body feel?
2. Describe that moment taking each sense in turn.

Variation 2: Staying Out, Going In
1. Choose a moment on your Story Map.
2. Think about the difference between what was happening on the surface and what was going on inside, in your mind and your body.
3. Describe the "outer" then the "inner" story.

MAKING LANGUAGE LIVE (*continued*)

Variation 3: Populating Your World

1. Look at your Story Map and the people in it. Choose one person.
2. Describe the person physically.
3. Describe the person's voice. What is he or she saying?
4. Describe your relationship to that person.

Variation 4: Comparing/Contrasting

1. Choose a moment on your Story Map that is particularly vivid for you.
2. Compare the moment to something else: "It was like..."

Hooks and Headlines

A hook is a phrase that dangles before you and gets your attention, teases you, grabs you and takes hold—just like a fishhook.

"Two years ago, I died on the operating table."

"My grandfather started Baskin-Robbins ice cream company."

Like a coat hook, it's a place for you to mentally hang things, a reminder of the theme or importance of a story.

"Getting locked up had set me free."

"Domestic violence thrives on silence."

Like the hook on a dress or a jacket, it fastens things, secures them in your mind so you repeat them to yourself and others.

"Cancer gave me membership to an elite club I'd rather not belong to."

"The containers they walk around with to carry water are the iPods of Africa. Every child has one."

And like a boxer's right hook, it can pack a wallop.

"We were told how much college would cost. I didn't realize it could cost me my son's life."

Hooks are ear-catching phrases that make you want to hear more or read on. They are so perfectly pithy, catchy, and crisp that they may capture the essence of your entire story in just a few choice words. When you lead off with a hook, it becomes a headline. Hooks help your audience remember key content and the theme of your story. They make it easy for audience members to tell others what was memorable about your story. In interviews, your hook may provide the interviewer with the title of the article or the quote that accompanies your photograph. It may help editors select which clip to use from your television, radio, or web interview.

Spend the time and challenge yourself to construct one, two, or three really good hooks. For ideas, look at your Six-Word Reason (page 26), your goals (page 52), your positive change (page 75), your key messages (page 58), and the following exercise.

EXERCISE

HOOK YOUR AUDIENCE

Objective: *Create ear-catching phrases*

Use this exercise to:
- Find memorable phrases that summarize your experience
- Discover other ways to express a key message

They're called *hooks* and *headlines* for a reason. Next time you're online, take note of the banner ads and the news summaries at the top of a webpage. When you

HOOK YOUR AUDIENCE (*continued*)

watch television, note the scrolling hooks at the bottom of the screen. Look at the attention-grabbers on magazine covers and listen to the teasers news anchors use just before commercial breaks; use these for inspiration in creating your own eye-catching, ear-pricking phrases.

The Exercise
- Here are five ideas for creating sparkling hooks. Feel free to base yours on the examples here.

1. Use a fact your audience may find intriguing or almost unbelievable.	
Two years ago, I died on the operating table. **Heart health advocate** My grandfather started Baskin-Robbins ice cream company. **Ocean Robbins, peace and environmental advocate**	**Try it:**

2. Repeat a key phrase to unify your story.	
I was the same person, but the world around me had changed... I hadn't changed as a person, the world around me had changed. **Rep. Tony Coelho, advocate for the Americans with Disabilities Act** Even those symptoms didn't get my attention ... the doctors weren't paying attention...pay attention and listen to your body. **Kathy Kastan, heart health advocate**	**Try it:**

101

HOOK YOUR AUDIENCE (*continued*)

3. Use analogies, metaphors and other poetic language to make direct or indirect comparisons.

Having cancer = "being a member in a club I'd rather not belong to." **Gilda Radner, comedian** The forty-pound Jerry cans children in Africa use to transport water = "the iPods of Africa." **Scott Harrison, advocate for clean drinking water** Domestic violence = a thing that thrives on silence. **Kristin Brumm, violence prevention advocate**	**Try it:**

4. Juxtapose two contrasting ideas.

We were told how much college would cost. I didn't realize it could cost me my son's life. **Deb, advocate for the National Meningitis Association** I had proudly served a country that was not proud of me. **Eric Alva, advocate for equity in the military** Getting locked up had set me free to create a life of meaning and purpose. **Gayathri Ramprasad, advocate for mental health**	**Try it:**

HOOK YOUR AUDIENCE (*continued*)

5. Use humor and wit—*if* it's appropriate to the setting and topic, *if* you know your audience, and *if* the humor comes naturally to you.

Help me make green the new black. Help me make sustainability sexy. **Majora Carter, advocate for environmental justice** My father learned that blood is thicker than ice cream. **Ocean Robbins, peace and environmental advocate (from the Baskin-Robbins ice cream family)**	**Try it:**

Chapter 6

Frame It

IN THIS CHAPTER:
- ❏ How to make your story come across in the way you want it to
- ❏ Working within the guidelines of a sponsoring organization

Providing Perspective

S uppose that your beloved three-year old niece or nephew draws a crayon masterpiece on a lunch bag. To display it, you could stick it on the refrigerator door with a magnet or place it in a modest black frame and add it to the family photo wall. Or … you might have it professionally framed: a museum-quality beveled matte under UV-protected glass, a blonde wood frame that is the perfect contrast to the child's wild use of Periwinkle and Burnt Sienna. Whatever display you choose will say something to viewers: "Isn't this cute?" or "This is not a scribble. This is serious artistic talent." Like the crayon drawing, your personal story can be framed many ways.

The idea that a framework can affect how we respond to something, or whether we even notice something, has proven useful in understanding how we communicate. The concept has been explored in linguistics, communication, sociology, political science, and the study

"Frames are mental structures that shape the way we see the world…the goals we seek, the plans we make, the way we act, and what counts as a good or bad outcome of our actions…. They are part of [our] cognitive unconscious— structures in our brains that we cannot consciously access, but know by their consequences: the way we reason and what counts as common sense. We also know frames through language."[1]

—George Lakoff

of social movements, and it is based on a simple analogy: just as a picture frame asks us to focus on whatever it surrounds, each of us creates *mental* frames that shape the way we see the world. Those mental frames are built upon our values and beliefs, and they operate very much like the frames around pictures: our minds focus only on what we want to see within that mental frame, ignoring or at least giving less attention to what is outside the border.

In our day-to-day conversation, we say things that let others know how we'd like our communication to be framed. If a friend tells you about something that happened to him yesterday and he begins with "Funny story: I was walking across the street when…," you probably understand he'd like you to use a comic frame to understand his story. When a neighbor stands up at a community meeting and passionately claims, "This is about accountability!" he has named a frame. A congresswoman debates legislation, saying, "This is not only about cutting costs, this is about justice." She too has named a frame. Each of these speakers uses *framing statements* to help others see what is or is not important to the discussion.

> **Framing statements put your story into context, situate it in terms of your advocacy goals, and highlight the values you hope to share with your audience.**

Why does framing matter when telling your story as an advocate? Because listeners may not automatically frame your story as you intend. You may need to include framing statements to help influence how listeners receive your story. Framing statements put your story into context, situate it among your advocacy goals, and highlight the values you hope to share with your audience. You may encourage understanding of different perspectives and potentially open up meaningful discussion by being clear about your own frames. Here are four important ways you might use in framing your story.

1. **Frame with values.** Name the core values that your story and your advocacy are built upon.
   – "This is about fairness."
   – "This is about taking personal responsibility."

2. **Frame with the theme or general topic**. Name the subject of your advocacy, the larger issue that your story speaks to.
   – "This is about access to sustainable modes of transportation."
   – "This is about the need for research funding."

3. **Frame by placing your story among other stories.** Help your audience make the bridge from your particular experience to the larger context.
   – "My story is only one of thousands."
   – "This is my experience. Other patients have different experiences."

4. **Frame with your desired outcome.** Remind the audience why you are sharing this story in this particular instance.
   – "I tell you my story with the hope that this never happens to other men and women in the armed forces."
   – "Remember that we're here because our children's safety matters."

> "This isn't just about me, this is a societal issue, this is a community issue. This is the story of thousands upon thousands of women. I'm talking about your sisters, your grandmothers, your aunts …"
>
> —**Kathy Kastan, heart health advocate**

Framing statements such as these help position how you would like the audience to view your story or the issue that you are advocating for. But framing statements operate in another important way: they can help influence how *you* are framed as a public advocate telling your personal story.

Every act of public communication is a presentation of self: whether consciously or unconsciously, we present ourselves in a manner that influences how others receive our messages. For example, we present ourselves confidently and professionally for a job interview (hopefully), compassionately and sincerely as a caregiver, resolutely and precisely as a legal defendant. Occasionally, depending on the situation, we may need to state overtly our desired presentation of self through *identity framing.*[2] Identity framing describes who we are as individuals or how we want to be perceived in a particular instance.

Why is identity framing particularly important when you tell your story as an advocate? Because when you share a personal story publicly, you present yourself as both message and messenger, story and storyteller; that's an inherent power of persuasive, personal storytelling. But if your audience is not open to your topic, to your organization, or even to the fact that you are sharing your personal story, they may frame you differently than you would like. Think of the words you would *not* want an audience to use to describe you as a storyteller or messenger: *whining, self-serving, just one person, victim…* To counter these perceptions, sometimes you may need to frame your identity clearly, plainly, and repeatedly.

> "Never be bullied into silence. Never allow yourself to be made a victim. Accept no one's definition of your life, but define yourself."
> —**Harvey Fierstein, actor and playwright**

Here are three important types of identity frames.

1. **Frame with your advocate identity.** Let the audience know
your relationship to this moment of advocacy.
   - "I'm an earth scientist, speaking on behalf of the Green House Initiative."
   - "I was asked to speak today and tell my story of..."
   - "I organized this event so we could share the stories ..."
   - "I am an advocate for..."

> "Stories do not simply describe the self; they are the self's medium of being."[3]
> —**Arthur W. Frank**

2. **Frame with a collective identity.** Name the larger
community that you are a part of or with which you hope
to make a difference. This may be your institutional,
professional, or cultural identity.
   - "I speak for all of us as concerned parents."
   - "As a member of this congregation..."
   - "I've been an employee here for 15 years."
   - "I'm an elected official, but I am also someone who..."
   - "As a third-generation member of this Polish community..."
   - "I am a Hmong American."
   - "I speak as a member of this city's LGBT elder community."

> "We're Iowans. We don't expect anyone to solve our problems for us. We'll fight our own battles. We just hope for equal and fair treatment from our government."[4]
> —**Zach Wahls, advocate for marriage equality**

3. **Frame with your storyteller identity.** Let the audience know how you view yourself *as someone who has had this experience.* In terms of "naming the change" (page 66), this is telling the audience who you are in the *Now* of your Story Map.
   – "I'm a survivor."
   – "I am witness to years of abuse."
   – "I am now a new person, one who..."

> "There are a lot of African-American males that are in special education but not many who make it out and who are successful. So I represent that population. And in special education, people with learning disabilities represent about 44%. So, I represent a large number of students."
> **—LeDerick Horne, advocate for people with disabilities**

Carey Christensen, an advocate for Parkinson's disease research and support, gives an example of why identity framing is particularly important to advocates who are telling their personal stories.

Carey was diagnosed with Parkinson's disease at the age of 41. As she set out to learn more about what she was experiencing and to find support, Carey became frustrated by how infrequently the voices of Parkinson's patients were part of the discussion. At the time, what she observed was that patients were being spoken to or spoken about, rather than being asked to speak for themselves.

That's when she stepped forward. From networking with other patients online, to connecting with a clinical researcher who helped tell her story of managing the psychological and neurological effects of the disease, to her current role as a patient advocate with the Michael J. Fox Foundation for Parkinson's Research, Carey has been clear about how she wants her story and her advocacy framed:

As Parkinson's patients, none of us wants to be hauled out there so people will say, "That poor person." We are telling our stories ourselves; that's where the switch has come in the advocacy movement. We have our own voices and we have our own stories to tell, and I am not going to let my caregiver tell it and I am not going to let the head of some foundation tell it. I am going to tell it: this is the reality, this is my life and this is how this disease has affected my life. My story is the most powerful thing I have and it is really precious to me. I want it presented correctly whenever I'm out there.

Because there is a reason I am telling this story; it is not just telling it for telling's sake, to get a pat on the head or to hear someone say, "I am so sorry." I am not looking for sympathy. I am looking for people to take action.

Deciding When to Frame or Reframe

Being aware of how framing works will help you in preparing for and making the most of speaking and interview situations.

As you think about where and how you'll share your story, you may decide that no additional framing is needed. For example, being interviewed for a local news segment titled "Stories of Hope" may not require you to frame your own story of hope. But frequently, you will need to frame or reframe your story so it is not misinterpreted, dismissed, or distorted. Here's how to be prepared.

Consider the Audience

How do you know what frames your audiences may carry? By considering their agenda and their values. By reflecting on their attitudes toward you, your story, and your advocacy goals. Use the Prep Sheets on pages 233 and 262, and the information in Chapters 7 and 8, to increase your sensitivity to audience perspectives.

Consider the Situation

Everything from the timing of your presentation or interview to the surrounding physical environment may determine whether framing is needed. It's particularly important to analyze the situation when you're preparing for media interviews. Often, a reporter, intentionally or not, may frame your story negatively, sensationally, or otherwise inappropriately.

The example on page 71 tells of an advocate for lung cancer awareness who inadvertently lets reporters frame his story as primarily one of grief and helplessness. See how we reframe his story as one of action and engagement on page 74. To explore speaking and interview situations, use the Prep Sheets on pages 233 and 262 and the information in Chapters 7 and 8.

Think about How People View Your Topic

Is the subject of your experience or advocacy a hot-button issue? Is it an everyday matter not typically seen as significant? Are there prevailing attitudes or beliefs in the air that you need to consider and respond to via an alternate frame? Might your audience have in mind other stories that go counter to your experience and the story you're going to tell? In Chapter 8 and in "Handling Questions from an Interviewer," (Chapter 14, page 260), read how to respond and reframe your story when it's framed inappropriately by others.

Lawrence Stallworth II, a twenty-three-year-old advocate for HIV/AIDS awareness who was diagnosed HIV-positive at age seventeen, has been speaking about living with HIV to a wide range of audiences: high school and college students, doctors and other members of the medical community, legislators and community members. With the stigma that still persists and the misperceptions about the virus and disease, Lawrence is particularly alert to how he and his story are framed. In one instance, he was invited to be part of an awareness event at a high school, sponsored jointly by a major cable television network and a philanthropic foundation. The panel consisted of a physician, Lawrence, and another HIV/AIDS advocate; three R&B recording artists, and a moderator who was a popular stand-up comedian. In recalling the event, Lawrence thought it could have gone better:

> In my opinion, the comic didn't show sensitivity to what it's like being a person with HIV. It wasn't anything offensive…a joke here and there. It was just that the event organizers didn't seem to be taking this as seriously as they should—considering they had people on this panel who were living with HIV. I learned a valuable lesson that day: Make sure organizers have the best interests in mind for you and your story.

Suppose you were in a situation like this, where your story was inappropriately framed by the mood and tone of an event. What might you say to reframe the situation before telling your story?

Working within Existing Frames and Guidelines

I n most cases, you will decide for yourself how and when to frame your story. But if you're working with an organization, sponsor, institution, or coalition, you may be "handed a frame" and asked to present your story in a particular light.

Advocacy groups, working at the grass roots or on the steps of government, rely on stories like yours to be a powerful part of their overall strategies; as such, you may need to frame accordingly. You may be asked to

- Emphasize a value that frames the issue strategically
- Highlight a theme or topic to keep the media focused on the sponsor's agenda
- Adopt a tone that reflects the collective identity
- Stress a desired outcome that is in line with the organization's mission and vision
- Identify your relationship to the organization, either as an official spokesperson or as an independent advocate

In certain cases, the goals and messages of your sponsoring organization may be determined—or constrained—by legal issues or government regulation. You'll likely need to stay within those guidelines or constraints, often referred to as guardrails, and you may need to take extra care in framing your story.

For example, suppose you're asked to share your story of an illness or health condition to an audience brought together by a pharmaceutical company that makes a treatment for that condition. The Food and Drug Administration, the governmental body regulating the pharmaceutical industry, requires the company and its spokespersons—in this case, you—to provide "fair balance" (similar to the disclaimers you hear or read in consumer advertisements for medicines and treatments). In other words, if your story is about how beneficial the treatment was to you, you may also need to remind the audience that "each person's case is unique," that "there are various side effects," and that "it's important to consult with your doctor." Other agencies, like the Federal Trade Commission, may also have requirements for transparency of sponsorship and disclosure of information in an interview.

Your sponsoring organization will inform you of these and other parameters so you can frame your story appropriately and share it with impact. It can be challenging at first to "mind the guardrails," but it helps you to focus and frame your story for the task at hand.

Use the following exercise, Build Your Frames, to provide the right perspective on your story.

EXERCISE

BUILD YOUR FRAMES

Objective: *Practice framing statements that help audiences view your story appropriately.*

Use this exercise to:
- Find useful framing statements
- Have ready-made responses to interview questions
- Be clear about what your story is and what it is not
- Be clear about how you want to be viewed in your story

There are a number of ways to build frames around stories or reframe them when necessary. This exercise has several options for you to try.

The Exercise
- Read the examples then try your hand at your own framing statements.

1. Frame with values. Name the core values that your story and the object of your advocacy are built upon.	
This is about *helping each other* change farming practices. I want to make sure other young people...have that *hope*, have that *opportunity*. ...That's what this bill is all about.	**My frames:**

2. Frame with the theme or general topic. Name the subject of your advocacy, the larger issue that your story speaks to.	
This is about protecting our youth. This is about how we need to be proactive patients.	**My frames:**

BUILD YOUR FRAMES *(continued)*

3. Frame by placing your story among other stories. Give your audience a bridge that connects your particular experience to the larger context.

My story is an all-too familiar one... Mine is another story of what a living wage really means...	**My frames:**

4. Frame with your desired outcome. Remind the audience why you are sharing your story in this particular instance.

I tell you this as an example of why we must not cut arts programs any further. I am living proof of the importance of early diagnosis.	**My frames:**

5. Frame with your identity as an advocate. Let the audience know your relationship to this moment of advocacy.

I am a WomenHeart Champion. I'm a major advocate of this legislation.	**My frames:**

119

BUILD YOUR FRAMES *(continued)*

6. Frame with a collective identity. Name the larger community that you are a part of or with whom you hope to make a difference.

Like many of you, I am the primary caregiver in our family... I speak as a proud member of this city's Latina community.	**My frames:**

7. Frame with your storyteller identity. Let the audience know how you view yourself *as someone who has had this experience.*

I am a survivor of colon cancer. I consider myself extremely fortunate to have been able to go through this.	**My frames:**

Chapter 7

Deliver Powerful Presentations

IN THIS CHAPTER:

❑ How to find the most useful attitude to be a confident, effective speaker

❑ Preparing for the audience, context, and physical environment

❑ Designing a strategic structure for your talk or presentation

From Informal Talks to Keynotes

An active and successful participant in high school debate, nineteen-year-old Zach Wahls was no stranger to public speaking when he gave testimony at the Iowa House of Representatives before a crowded audience of politicians, citizens, and TV cameras. But it was the first time he stood up and told his personal story and, like other advocates, he found that preparing to speak a personal truth publicly was a whole new ballgame: "It took me a couple of months to find the courage to actually come forward and talk about my family, first in writing, then speaking at the Iowa House." Though initially overwhelmed at the thought of speaking about a complex and often contentious issue like marriage equality, Zach received smart advice from friends: "Focus on what you know. Talk about your family." He thought, "Okay, well…I can do that"— and he began drafting his remarks.

The term *public speaking* usually calls to mind a setting similar to the one in which Zach spoke: a person stands at a lectern before a seated audience, often with some projected visual aids on a screen behind. You may tell your story in this traditional, formal speaking situation if you're a guest or keynote speaker at an

> "What goes on at the growing edges of life is seldom written down at the time. It is lived from day to day in talk. In scraps of comment on the margins of someone else's manuscript, in words spoken on a street corner…."[1]
>
> —**Margaret Mead**

event or providing legal testimony, but other settings may be very informal—like the one in which Theresa Greenleaf told her story.

When Theresa's son Jack was in the third grade, there was a younger boy at his school with a severe allergy to peanuts. On two separate occasions, he had such strong reactions to food he came in contact with that paramedics were called to the school. To guard against this happening again, the school nurse, Wendy, sent a note to the boy's homeroom parents asking them to refrain from packing peanut butter sandwiches or other nut products in lunches. Some of the parents didn't respond well to the request. At the time, Theresa says, there wasn't a great understanding of how serious allergic reactions or asthma attacks could be.

To increase awareness and persuade the parents to comply with the request, Nurse Wendy scheduled a meeting with the parents, invited an allergist to speak, and asked a few parents of children with allergies to tell their stories. Theresa's son Jack had food allergies and asthma, so she had valuable experiences to share. She remembers:

Wendy was really smart about how she approached this. The meeting was in the school library, with a very intimate feel. It wasn't like she brought a parade of parents up to a podium to speak at the other parents. We just sat together; we were parents among parents.

With my story I wanted to emphasize that it can be really scary—and you learn that you need to rely on and trust other parents and caregivers. I told what I had gone through trying to keep Jack's environment allergen-free. I told some of the scary stories and I told the absolute worst story: when I was taking him to the doctor with an asthma episode and he lost consciousness in the cab. I was already doing all kinds of stuff, I was leaving no stone unturned and even then—this happened. I talked about the ongoing effort and how appreciative I was of all the support I got from the school and other parents. I framed it in the light of appreciation.

Whether you're sitting in a grade school library, standing at a lectern, or canvassing door-to-door, it's all *public speaking*. And in every situation, your objective is the same: to be confident, comfortable, and clear as you tell your story *and* deliver your messages.

Some people have a natural gift for public speaking; most of us require guidance and practice. But a little guidance and practice goes a long way in helping you feel more comfortable and confident in public speaking situations. Becoming an effective communicator is an ongoing process, and the best advocates will tell you they never stop learning or looking for ways to improve. Regardless of how you feel right now about speaking out—whether you're "eager but anxious" or "committed and confident"—remember these three golden rules:

"I gave a talk at a local Baptist Church. There were probably thirty women in the room; I didn't think it went that well. But after I finished, this woman came up to me and she said, 'In my life I have never heard a speech so powerful.' Months later she told me she had quit smoking. She'd been smoking for 40 years. She quit smoking, and has not picked up a cigarette since. Well, I didn't even think that much of my presentation. But you can change people's lives without even knowing you're doing it."

—**Kathy Kastan,
heart health advocate**

1. Every opportunity to speak is an opportunity for growth.
2. Growth comes from setting goals—and forgiving the moments when you don't hit them.
3. Most public speaking anxieties are taken care of when you know what you want to say, why you're saying it, and to whom.

Use the principles in this chapter and Chapter 13 (Public Speaking: Tips and Tools, page 221) as you get ready to speak. Talk to other advocates about what they've learned and the powerful experiences they've had connecting with audiences. When you're ready, turn to the Seven Practice Runs in Chapter 9 to prepare for your next speaking opportunity.

Being Audience-Centered

W hether they're getting ready to speak to a roaring crowd or to a single person, the best advocates know that an important step in preparation is the one that takes them *outside* of themselves so they can consider the audience's perspective. Being audience-centered means finding out as much as you can about the audience—their attitudes, values, moods, knowledge— then tailoring what you say accordingly. It does *not* mean pandering to the audience or subordinating your own goals and passions. Being audience-centered simply means you've thought about how to best reach your audience so you communicate *with* them rather than talk *at* them.

> **Being audience-centered enables you to define how far you are asking your audience to journey with you to reach your advocacy goal.**

Perhaps most importantly, being audience-centered helps you determine where your audience stands on the issue you're advocating. Are they already supportive and familiar with your cause, or are they unfamiliar, unaware, or even resistant to the change you're advocating? Remember that advocacy is a persuasive act; you have a goal or goals to achieve by telling your story. You want your audience to *do something*—whether that something is becoming more aware of an issue, considering their own attitudes or behaviors, or joining you in taking up a fight. Being audience-centered enables you to define how far you are asking your audience to journey with you to reach your advocacy goal.

Look again at the illustration below. What are you hoping your audience will do, specifically, because they've heard your story?

When you know your audience, you know what story to tell. You know whether framing or reframing is necessary. And you stay focused on your key messages and goals. When you're

Real Audiences Wear Clothes

You've probably heard the advice to practice speaking in front of a mirror or to imagine the audience in their underwear to calm your nerves. While a mirror's always helpful to check your appearance or see what a gesture looks like, don't get stuck there. When you get up in front of an audience you won't be speaking to your reflection, you'll be speaking to actual humans. And chances are they'll be clothed. Imagine your audience as they'll show up and *you'll* show up more comfortably.

audience-centered, you can anticipate both the challenges and opportunities of any speaking situation.

And there's one more benefit to being audience-centered: the more you know about your audience and the more clearly you can visualize them as you prepare, the more confident and natural you'll be when you speak. Most of the anxiety we feel about speaking comes from fear of the unknown: "What if they don't get it? What if they don't like it? What if they can't hear me?" Taking the time to address these questions and getting to know

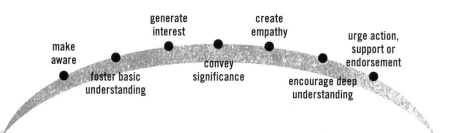

make aware • foster basic understanding • generate interest • convey significance • create empathy • encourage deep understanding • urge action, support or endorsement

your audience *as you prepare* removes layer after layer of anxiety, helping you show up as your best self.

How much information you can gather about an audience depends on the time you have to prepare and the access you have to the audience. You certainly can't know everything, and you'll have to make some assumptions. Still, gather as much information as you can to make those assumptions as accurate as possible— through observation, contact with others, or research. Here are some ways to gather this important information:

- **Ask.** If you're invited to speak, contact the organizers before the event. Ask if they would answer a few questions about the audience.
- **Reach out.** Contact other speakers who've addressed this audience.
- **Search online.** If the audience members belong to a group or organization, visit the group's website or read its published materials.
- **Watch.** Stand at the door and greet people as they arrive, or position yourself so you can observe the audience and gauge their moods.

Use the Speaking Prep Sheet, "Prepare for Your Audience," in Chapter 13 (page 233) as a guide to the kinds of information you can gather to create a full portrait of the audience. This includes information like demographics (Who are they? What ages, genders, and cultural backgrounds are represented?), situation (Why are they here? How large is the audience? Is the setting formal or informal?), attitudes (How might they feel about you, your topic, and your story? What do they expect to hear? What's their level of interest? What level of disclosure is appropriate?) and values (How do they think? What's important to them? What will seem familiar to them? What will seem foreign?).

Being audience-centered helped Theresa Greenleaf anticipate how other parents might respond to her story. It also helped her focus on what, specifically, she wanted to achieve:

I knew I had to be very careful of not painting a portrait of mothers of kids with allergies and asthma as being overprotective nut jobs. I also knew that I didn't want to "apologize," like when you make other parents or teachers aware that your child has the potential for anaphylactic shock and you get into that "Oh, gee. I'm sorry to have to tell you—I'm sorry that this is a potential pain in the neck."

What I really wanted to do was bring them into that cab with me, to share the moment of nearly losing my child—to have them reflect on the reality of this situation.

> "I had never shared my story of mental illness in class, but my professor was very supportive. I was literally shaking as I presented the 5-minute speech…but was absolutely bowled over by the response. Every one of my fellow students said either they had struggled with mental illness or they knew somebody in their family or their circles of friends and colleagues who had. The responses to that first speech empowered me to invest the rest of my life in what I'm doing now as an advocate."
> —**Gayathri Ramprasad, mental health advocate**

The Speaking Context

Many factors can define a particular speaking context, ranging from how you came to be there to the function your story is asked to fulfill to the time of day and what's going on in the news. All of these can affect how you tell your story and how it's received. Being aware of the speaking context means stepping back and surveying the lay of the land. In this section, we'll consider some of the factors that determine speaking context.

Timing

Some say it's everything. At what time during the day are you telling your story, and where are you on the agenda? Where does your story fall in an awareness-raising campaign or in relation to what's going on in the news?

All of these timing factors can affect how your audience hears and responds to you, and they may require you to acknowledge the timing of your presentation. For example, a hot news story that relates to yours may give you the perfect introduction. How your story relates to other stories on the agenda also may be worth noting.

Your Role

Each speaking situation may require something different from you. What you say and how you say it will depend upon your role and responsibilities, so ask yourself, "What is being asked of me in this particular situation?" Then address more specific questions, such as:

- What is the event or occasion? What's the mood?
- Am I the primary speaker? Am I responsible for saying anything in addition to my story? Who else will be speaking?
- What role is my story being asked to play in this event? When will I tell my story?

Framing

Your presentation or talk will be framed in various ways: by what happens right before and after you speak, by how you are introduced, or even by a banner hanging behind you. These contextual elements may provide the perfect frame to your story. Or they may create a context that is wrong for your talk, requiring you to reframe with statements that help the audience receive your story as you intend (see Chapter 6: Frame It).

Environment

Whether you're speaking in a hotel ballroom, in the town square, or in a grade school library, any physical environment presents both opportunities and challenges to telling your story effectively. The best way to know how you can make an environment work for you is to get an early look at it. Many of the challenges of a

> "The fundraising event was the first time I told my story in a public speech. The only other times I'd spoken before was professionally, when I had been more removed from the audience, like on a stage, where I was not able to look at them eye-to-eye. Speaking at the fundraiser in the living room, everybody was right there. And anywhere I turned I could see every facial expression, not that far away from me. This was totally different."
>
> **—Derek Cotton, advocate for cancer support services**

131

speaking environment can be eliminated with a little foresight and some minor adjustments, though others may require you to adapt on the fly. Here are some tips for managing the opportunities and challenges of the physical environment.

- **Be your audience.** Use your audience-centered perspective and literally put yourself in the audience's position. Sit or stand where the audience will be.

- **Reduce distractions.** Look for potential barriers or interrupters: the mirrored wall behind the speaker's lectern, the noisy schoolyard next door, the large column in the middle of the room. What draws your attention?

- **Set the stage.** A large hotel ballroom with lighting, stage, microphone, and lectern suggests a degree of formality you may want. But will your talk to a small group in the community center require the same arrangements? Possibly not. You may decide that sitting in a circle is more conducive—as Nurse Wendy knew when she set the stage for the "parents among parents" in the school library.

- **If you don't like it, change it.** Consider how much control you have over the physical environment and aspects of the context, such as timing or framing. You may find you have more control than you thought. Be proactive in making the speaking situation work best for you, your story, and your audience. Move that lectern, use that poster as a backdrop, suggest speaking before or after the break, or find out how you will be introduced.

Use the Prep Sheets in Chapter 13 (starting on page 233) to assess the speaking context and aspects of the physical environment.

Strategic by Design

The types of talks or presentations you give as an advocate can vary greatly. What you say will depend on your goals, your responsibilities, the audience, and the context.

Sometimes, for example, you're asked to "just tell" your story, perhaps at an event where other speakers will be responsible for giving information about their organization and explaining the advocacy goal. This was the case when Theresa Greenleaf spoke in the grade school library, joined by an allergist and the school nurse. Her charge was to provide living proof that attention to allergens was a serious issue.

At other times, you may be responsible not only for telling your story but also for speaking about the cause, organization, or campaign. In Kathy Kastan's address at a fundraiser for the Cardiovascular Research Foundation (page 145), she served as a keynote speaker who was asked to share her story of heart disease, to talk about the organization she represented, and to stress the importance of increased attention to women's heart health. On page 145, you'll see how Kathy organized her presentation to meet her specific goals, stress her key messages, and move the audience to action. While Theresa's talk to parents in the school library was in a much more casual context, it was just as important for her to consider how she would structure her communication.

On one hand, the structure of your talk or presentation is purely functional: it provides clarity and order, and it gives your audience a way of making sense of your story and messages. But because advocacy is a persuasive act, structure is also strategic. The structure should help you reach your advocacy goals by moving your audience to action, whether that structure is loose or tight, highly conceptual or carefully plotted.

Whether you're "just telling" your story or telling your story *and* conveying other substantial information, all of your talks or presentations should be built on the same basic framework: introduction, body, and conclusion. This is the skeleton of any effective communication. How you actually build your talk or presentation upon this skeleton is one of the most creative aspects of public speaking. We'll offer you a few options for how you might do this, but let's first look at the essential elements of an intro, body, and conclusion.

The Introduction

Compared to the rest of your presentation, the introduction is short. It may only be a couple sentences. At minimum, an introduction should do the following things:

- **Gain and focus your audience's attention.** This may be a simple pause before you begin, a moment of interaction with your audience, or a scene from your story. It might be your headline or a hook. Be creative, but make sure your attention-getter is appropriate to your cause, the occasion, and your individual speaking style.
- **Establish your purpose for speaking.** This may be a framing statement ("I'm here as a representative of . . ."), a clear assertion of your goal ("I'm happy to share what this

program has meant to me and my family") or what you
intend for your audience ("This is information important to
your health and well-being").

- **Preview your structure or key points.** If giving a
  presentation is like taking the audience on a journey, then
  the preview is where you first spread the map out on the
  table, point out the stops along the way, and describe the
  final destination. Your preview may be general ("Here's what
  my experience with the legal system has been and why I
  believe this change in policy is needed.") or specific ("I'll
  share four things you can do right now to help combat
  this stigma.").

The Body

The body is the substance of your talk or presentation and the
longest section. Depending upon the speaking context and
your role, the body may consist primarily of your story and key
messages, or it may cover additional content such as information
about your sponsoring organization or the larger advocacy efforts.
Compared to the intro and conclusion, the body has the most
flexibility for creative and strategic organization.

The Conclusion

Like the introduction, the conclusion is brief. At minimum,
it should:

- **Remind the audience of the key messages.** Make the most
  of this, your last chance to create an impact. Audiences
  remember final words; make them memorable. "Bookend"
  your talk, by relating your conclusion back to your
  introduction. Perhaps repeat your framing statement or goal.

- **Present any "calls to action."** Tell your audience specifically what you want them to do after listening to you. Think about the behavior you want to affect and where on the spectrum of persuasion that action falls.

Organizational Options

The intro, body, and conclusion serve as the underlying structure for any advocacy presentation: long or short, formal or informal, talk or keynote. But there are many ways you might organize your body of content to achieve your specific advocacy goals.

In this section, we'll look at a few options. Some are conceptual approaches to how you weave your story in and around the key messages and supporting material. Others are detailed "recipes" for moving audiences to action. Note that in every case, you still need to meet the essential requirements of an intro and conclusion.

Story as Backbone

Use your story as the spine of the body, bringing in key messages or supporting material as appropriate.

Here are some tips:

- Look to your Story Map to find moments you can link to the key messages that you or your organization want to convey.
- Make the links between your story and key messages explicit. State them clearly. Don't cross your fingers and hope your audience will "get it."
- Use the exercise on page 60 (Link to Key Messages) to build this structure.

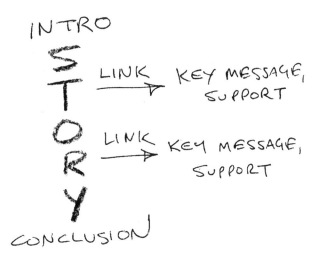

Story as Proof Point

Use your story to support the key messages and other content. This structure is useful when your main goal is to introduce an audience to an organization or issue.

Here are some tips:

- It's often helpful to focus first on the key messages and supporting material, then look to your story for proof points.
- If you speak frequently as an advocate for your organization—as its director, board president, or media spokesperson—this is a handy template.

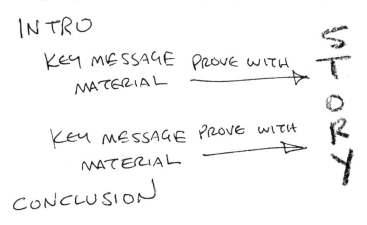

Story as Envelope

Begin and end with your story, using it as the "wrapping" that contains your key messages and other content. This approach is useful for creating suspense (How does the story end?), naming the change that happened in you, and establishing your credibility right off the bat.

Here's a tip:

• When you return to your story at the end of your talk, you may need to remind the audience where you left off before continuing.

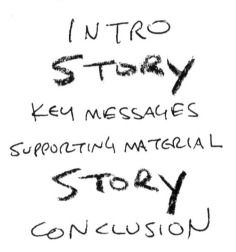

Landing Points

This circular approach enables you to "wrap up the package" by showing how important moments in your story or supporting information lead you back to the main idea. A "landing point" may be a critical moment in your story, a key message, the most startling statistic, or a moment of interaction with the audience.

Here are some tips:

• Look to your hooks and headlines, your Six-Word Reason, or the specific goal of your talk for the main idea.

- This is handy organization if you don't have much time to prepare and you have to give a more impromptu talk. Use the landing points to keep yourself on track; you'll know where you want to land and where you want to end up… how you get there may vary!

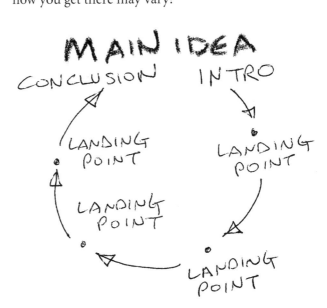

The Change Journey

This structure focuses on the change that occurred in you and the change you want to see (Chapter 4: Point to the Positive). Take the audience on the journey of your experience, but stop along the way to explain insights, challenges, and lessons learned, as well as to deliver key messages.

Here are some tips:

- Remember to tell both inner and outer stories (page 95).
- If certain moments are still too emotionally charged for you, rethink what you want to tell and how you will tell it.

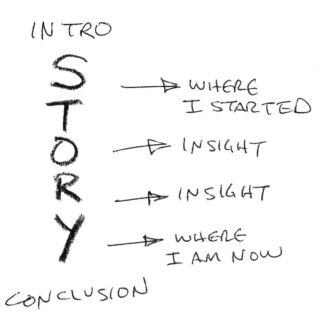

INTRO

STORY
- WHERE I STARTED
- INSIGHT
- INSIGHT
- WHERE I AM NOW

CONCLUSION

Problem–Solution

This simple persuasive structure divides your talk or presentation into two sections—the problem and the solution. The solution is typically the course of action you want your audience to take, endorse, or consider. How you incorporate your story depends on what kind of "living proof" it provides. Is your experience proof that there is a problem, or is your story proof that there is a solution (or both)?

Here are some tips:

- Remember to give your audience a clear call to action. Say what it is you hope they will do.
- Consider the spectrum of persuasion (page 51) and where your audience stands in relation to the solution you offer.

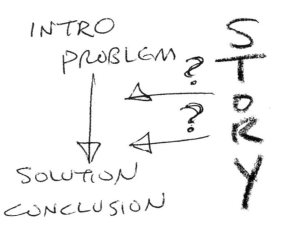

The organizations just described offer you some general and fairly flexible approaches. These next two are more prescriptive "recipes."

Brief, Brisk Blueprint

This simple organization is useful if you're telling your story to legislators—one of the most effective ways to affect public policy on an issue. Public officials are generally eager to meet with their constituents, but there are many people competing for their time. So when you or your sponsoring organization secure a face-to-face meeting with a legislator, it's critical to use your time—which will be brief—very wisely. Use this brief, brisk blueprint—and the fundamentals laid out in *Living Proof*—to stay on point and tell a powerful story.

1. **Introduce yourself and frame.** Say who you are, why you are advocating for this issue, and then frame your talk (see framing statements, page 107).

2. **Tell your story.** Summarize your story, then zero in on a powerful moment (see "Adjusting the Pace" in Chapter 5, page 86).

3. **Link your story to the policy objective.** Demonstrate that your story is living proof of positive impact (see Chapter 4: Point to the Positive).

4. **Make a clear ask.** State simply and succinctly what you hope the legislator does or supports.

5. **Thank.** Thank the official for her time. Follow up with a written thank-you that mentions your story ("Thank you for allowing me to share the story of my son Ryan and his experience in middle school").

Monroe's Motivated Sequence

Here's a tried-and-true persuasive formula for moving an audience to act. Dr. Allen Monroe of the University of Chicago popularized this five-step model in the 1940s. Next time you watch television or online media, notice how many commercials still follow this structure. A good example of this sequence in action is Scott Harrison's speech at the Big Omaha tech conference (Chapter 5, page 146).

1. **Attention.** As in any good introduction, start by gaining the audience's attention by relating the topic directly to them.

2. **Need.** Make the audience feel the need for a positive change. Focus on how your information or story demonstrates a serious problem. In addition to your story, use strong supporting materials—statistics, visuals, quotes from others. By the time you finish this step, listeners should be deeply concerned and ready to hear your solutions.

3. **Satisfaction.** Provide a solution to the problem, and map out the positive change you're advocating. Depending on the context, you may present detailed information, showing how the solution will work.

4. Visualization. An important step: have your audience visualize the benefits of your plan. This is where you use vivid imagery to illustrate that better world you advocate, helping the audience *see* how much better it will be once that positive change has been achieved.

5. Action. Say exactly what you want the audience to do, and tell them how they should go about doing it. Remind them once more of the seriousness of the problem and the need for change.

Use the Speaking Prep Sheets in Chapter 13. Start with "The Basic Structure" on page 239 to plan the foundation of your next presentation, or use the ones on the subsequent pages 240-248 to try other structures.

Ready to practice? Use the Practice Runs exercise in Chapter 9 to get ready for your next talk.

Examples

Story as Envelope

Here's how heart health advocate Kathy Kastan used the Story as Envelope structure for her address at a fundraiser for the Cardiovascular Research Foundation.

Introduction	
• Grab and focus audience attention	Kathy began with a hook and the theme of her presentation: "At 41, I never thought about my own mortality. My attention was elsewhere. When I started having shortness of breath, fatigue, pain in my upper left back, and occasional pain down my left arm, I noticed that something was changing in my body. But even having those symptoms off and on for 8 months didn't get me to pay attention. Nor did I tell anyone."
• Establish your purpose • Preview your story or key messages	"How many of you truly pay attention to your bodies, your emotions, and your health?"
Body	
• Tell your crafted, *focused story*	Kathy used her story as the "envelope," taking her audience through her journey of unrecognized symptoms of heart disease, misdiagnosis, correct diagnosis, bypass surgery, and return to health. Throughout, she echoed her main theme: "And then one day while I was on vacation in the majestic Colorado Rockies I collapsed on a sidewalk with not vague symptoms but classic Hollywood heart attack symptoms (front to back chest pain etc.). Well, that got my attention. It got my husband's attention too. I went to a second cardiologist who confirmed that I had been misdiagnosed but unfortunately he really wasn't paying attention either and sent me on my way. It wasn't until I collapsed a second time that I got his attention." After delivering supporting material about heart disease in women and her sponsoring organization, Kathy returned to her story to stress the importance of "paying attention."

Conclusion	
• Remind the audience of your key messages • Present any "call to action"	Kathy gave her audience a number of ways to "pay attention," including knowing the risks of heart disease and visiting the website of the organization she represented.

Monroe's Motivated Sequence

At a meeting of movers and shakers on the "Silicon Prairie" called Big Omaha, Scott Harrison told the story of how he founded the organization charity: water with the goal of bringing clean drinking water to billions. The conference audience of five hundred was already supportive and sympathetic, having contributed $5,000 for the organization before the conference. Using personal experience and moving photographs to tell the story of his organization, Scott motivated the audience to do more. Following his presentation, another $10,000 was contributed. You can find a link to Scott's 45-minute presentation at www. livingproofadvocacy.com/blog/resources. Here's how he fulfilled Monroe's five steps.

Attention	
Gain the audience's attention. Relate the topic directly to the audience.	Everyone knew Scott was there to talk about water and his organization. He thanks them for the $5,000 they've raised, telling how it would be used. Then he surprises them: 　"I'm going to start by first telling you about my mother." He tells of his childhood, caring for his mother who had a compromised immune system, and of his rebellion at age 18: 　"I spent my life looking after her, now it was time to look out for Number One. Grew my hair long, joined a band, moved to New York City. I wanted to be rich and famous and I wanted to do all the things I was told I wasn't able to do. And I got really good at that."

	We follow him from his "selfish and arrogant" life as a nightclub promoter to his feelings of spiritual bankruptcy to his volunteering for a humanitarian organization offering free medical care in Africa, where: "I got my first taste of dirty water in Liberia."
Need Make the audience feel the need for a positive change.	He tells why he decided to focus his new, charitable self on water issues: "… one of the most important issues facing the poor today. It was connected to so many other things I'd seen. It was a root cause. It was the reason kids weren't able to get an education." Graphically, both visually and verbally, Scott relates story after story of what he saw in West Africa. Statistics, video of parasites in drinking water, stories of families carrying 40-pound Jerry cans of contaminated water, and teenage girls whose lives are defined by deficiency: "…kids grow up and their spines are bent 'cause they started carrying water at the age of 5."
Satisfaction Provide a solution to the problem; map out the positive change for which you advocate.	With the audience primed for a solution, he says: "The good news is that there are solutions and we know how to help a billion people." He shows the kinds of solutions that charity: water has funded: wells, filters, rainwater catchment. He tells how the wells are built, tells stories of the local community rallying around the projects. He reminds the audience that the $5,000 they raised paid for the drilling of wells, and each one provides water for more than 250 people.
Visualization Have your audience visualize the benefits of your plan.	With his key message that "water is everything," Scott vividly shows what happens when a community gets clean water: "It's awesome when you hit water. It's one of the greatest things…water really changes everything. We believe this to our core. Clean water brings hope into communities, it brings life. It restores dignity to women, to kids, to teenage girls. It puts so much time back into the community. Disease rates start plummeting when clean water is brought into a community. And we can prove it. And we can show it can be done." Scott then tells how charity: water came to be, their fundraising strategies, their successes, their mistakes. And—most importantly—he tells stories of how individuals have creatively raised money: from

	kids "giving up their birthdays" to four guys walking across the United States to "Jodie Landers, a mom from Muscatine, Iowa. She adopted two kids from Sierra Leone, went to her church, went to schools, said, "Kids around the world need clean water." Raised $300,000 in her small town."
Action Say exactly what you want the audience to do and how they should go about doing it.	Briefly and succinctly: "So I'd like to ask you guys: will you make this your story? What can you do to help? Some of you can get your companies involved. Everyone in this room could give up a birthday." Visibly moved, he concludes: "If not us, who? And if not now, when?"[2]

Chapter 8

Give Great Interviews

IN THIS CHAPTER:

❏ How to take all the opportunities offered by a media interview
❏ Getting to know your target audience
❏ Preparing for the interview context
❏ How to amaze your friends and family with your media skills

The Media Opportunity

As an advocate, you have the *one* thing every reporter, blogger, and journalist wants. You have a story. You have a story that's been crafted to be engaging and memorable, a story told genuinely with the audience in mind. This is precisely what media interviewers look for because what they fear most is that they'll speak to someone who is unprepared and unresponsive. That's not you.

You just need to make sure the story you tell is the one the reporter reports.

From start to finish—from taking a media call to the wrap-up question and last few seconds of a broadcast—interviews are about opportunity. Advocates sometimes dodge media interviews because they assume the reporter will be a barrier to delivering their messages or story. While it's true some interviews can be challenging, in most instances you and the reporter are focused on the very same goal: a compelling story. An interview is a wide expanse of opportunity, not a minefield. To give a great interview, you need to be prepared and alert, ready to seize every moment of what will likely be a very short time.

> **From start to finish— from taking a media call to the wrap-up question and last few seconds of a broadcast—interviews are about opportunity.**

Before becoming an advocate for stricter laws against distracted driving, Loren Vaillancourt was uncomfortable with any type of public speaking. Her brother's death in a car crash changed that:

Right after Kelson was killed, it was so strange, because I had this overwhelming feeling that I had to tell his story, and I had to do it for him, and that I could possibly save lives. It wasn't the easiest thing to accept right away, to be honest with you, because—good gracious—I never in a million years could see myself doing as much speaking as I am.

It wasn't long, however, before Loren found herself speaking frequently to local and national media. As the reigning Miss South Dakota, Loren gave reporters a compelling angle: a pageant queen with an intimate perspective on an issue getting national attention. With her key message that "These accidents are 100 percent preventable," Loren gave audiences a very effective advocacy story: focused, crafted, framed, practiced, and pointing to positive change. Her 3.5-minute appearance on a national CBS morning show is a great example of the opportunity in a media interview. View the segment at www.livingproofadvocacy.com/blog/resources.

As with any type of successful communication, giving a great interview is a matter of anticipation and preparation. First, you want to know your audience so you can keep them firmly in mind. Next, you'll need to assess the interview context by knowing the type of interview, the setting, and the interviewer. Then, applying some basic media skills, give the reporter a story that not only reaches and moves audiences but also advances your advocacy mission.

Use the principles in this chapter and Chapter 14 (Media Interviews: Tips and Tools, page 249) as you get ready for your interview. Watch other advocates like Loren online and on television to see how the best speakers make it look natural. When you're ready, use the Seven Practice Runs exercise in Chapter 9 to get ready for your next media opportunity.

Know Your Target Audience

W hen you give a presentation, you have direct access to your audience—the people who watch, listen, and respond to you.

SPEAKER ⟶ AUDIENCE

In media interviews, you rarely have direct access to your audience. The interviewer *serves as a conduit, sometimes a filter* that your messages pass through to reach the viewers, listeners, or readers.

SPEAKER ⟶ INTERVIEWER ⟶ AUDIENCE

Your target audience—made up of media consumers—is where you want to focus: on the people who listen to the news or podcast, pick up the magazine, or watch the talk show. Knowing your target audience is vital to deciding how you tell your story and what key messages you stress. Build a mental image of your target audience by gathering as much information as you can about why they'll be interested in what you have to say. Here are some ideas of how to gather information about your target audience.

- **Preview.** If you're being interviewed for TV, radio, or the Internet, you can preview the show or blog to see how the media outlet speaks to the target audience and what they report on. Look online for archived videos or audio interviews, especially those related to your topic.

- **Read.** For a print piece, read the articles by the reporter who's interviewing you and review past issues of the magazine or newspaper (often available online).

- **Surf.** Visit the media outlet's website. Look under "Advertise with Us," and you may find a summary of the target audience (median age, gender, education, and interests).

- **Test.** Do you know some people who read, watch, or listen to the media outlet that will interview you? Try out your story and key messages on them. Ask what they like best about the media.

Use the Interview Prep Sheet, "Prepare for Your Audience," on page 262 as a guide to the kind of information you can gather to paint a picture of your target audience: demographics (Who are they? How do they engage with this media outlet?), interests (Why are they interested in this media, this topic?), and attitudes (How might they feel about you, your topic, or your story?).

The Interview Context

The typical interview situation is one that supports your message of positive change. These human-interest articles or public service segments may promote an upcoming event, feature a hometown angle, or be part of a large awareness or education campaign. The tone of these interviews is positive, and the interviewer allows you to tell your story well and deliver key messages clearly. When Loren Vaillancourt appeared on *The Early Show*, the news anchor cast Loren's story as important living proof of the need for stricter laws, opening with "There's a troubling new report out this morning about distracted driving," and closing with "All it takes is a split second for you to remove your eyes from the road." All Loren needed to provide was the evidence her compelling story illustrated.[1]

But many factors can affect how the dynamics of an interview play out, so as you prepare it's important to step back and consider the wider context. Think of it as finding out what direction the river is flowing, and at what speed, before you push off from shore in your kayak, with paddle ready.

- What is the reason for the interview?
- What is the focus of the interview?
- What information am I responsible for conveying? Are there organizational messages I must deliver?
- How do I want my story to be framed?

An array of factors will determine the interview context. Here are five of them:

1. **Timing**. In Loren's case, the timing was perfect. Her interview aired the same day the Department of Transportation launched a major awareness campaign on the dangers of distracted driving. But depending on the nature of your cause and what else is happening in the world of news, the interview atmosphere may be less than supportive. Your topic or the organization you represent may be considered controversial by the media, and the reporter may look to challenge you. Popular attitudes toward your topic may influence the reporter's stance and the questions asked.

2. **Your role**. Suppose, for example, that you are being interviewed as an official spokesperson. You may be responsible for delivering organizational messages, which may include restrictions on what you can and cannot say. See "Working within Existing Frames and Guidelines" in Chapter 6 (page 116).

3. **The reporter**. Reporters come in all shapes and sizes, personality types, and skill levels. They may know quite a bit about your topic, or they may arrive unprepared. But they have one thing in common: they're under pressure to capture a good story, on deadline. To help reporters get what they want, on time, see "Handling Questions from an Interviewer" in Chapter 14 (page 260).

4. **Framing**. How the media frames your story may or may not match how you want it to be framed. Your story may be framed as confident advocacy or hesitant disclosure. You may be framed as a fierce crusader or a tragic victim. Loren

Vaillancourt *could* have been framed many ways in her media appearance: grieving sister, Miss America contestant, angered survivor. Instead, though, the news anchor framed Loren as a dedicated advocate: "You're out there speaking to people about this all the time. Do you feel like being out there, speaking out about it…is that making an impact?"

5. **Form of media**. Print, television, web, or radio—each form requires certain skills and special attention to how you present yourself and your story. Each form also changes the dynamic between you and the reporter, as well as you and your target audience.

Use Chapter 14, Media Interviews: Tips and Tools (page 249), to assess and manage the interview context, as well as to prepare for radio, television, web, and print interviews.

157

Staying in Your Story and on Message

You know your story, your key messages, and who your target audience is. Now it's time to practice some fundamental interview techniques to ensure that, no matter how an interview goes, no matter what questions a reporter asks, you'll be able to tell your story powerfully and make your points clearly.

A media interview—whether for print or broadcast—is not a simple question-and-answer exchange between you and a reporter. It's not a conversation—although it should sound like one—nor an interrogation. It's an opportunity for you to deliver specific messages to specific audiences through the filter of a reporter. Think of the interview process as talking *through* the reporter to your audience.

"A skill I've learned throughout the year with my media appearances is to come up with a 5-minute version. And then a 1-minute version. And then a 30-second version. And then a 10-second version. So no matter what kind of environment you're put in, you're always able to get the most important points across."

—Loren Vaillancourt, advocate for stricter distracted driving laws

You were probably contacted by or asked to speak to the media because you have a story to tell, so reporters will often ask questions that let you get quickly to your story. But you can't always count on the right questions being asked. Even if you have

QUESTION → RESPONSE → QUESTION → RESPONSE

INTERVIEWER IN CONTROL

a good idea of the kinds of questions a reporter may ask, you won't know exactly *how* they'll be asked. So don't head into an interview hoping and waiting for the right questions. If you passively engage with an interviewer, simply responding to the questions, you risk giving him or her complete control over the interview's direction. In extreme cases, when a reporter has a particular agenda that is counter to yours, being a passive interviewee allows the reporter to put together a story quite different from yours. (See the example on page 71.)

Instead, actively participate in the interview, viewing each question as an opportunity to tell your story and deliver your messages.

> "When I finally made the decision to tell my domestic violence story to the media, I was firmly strategic about it. I was very clear on what my main points were, what I would say, what I would not say, where I would not let the conversation go. I was clear that this was a story about safety. And it paid off. They were extremely cooperative. They understood the gravity of the situation and they were very respectful of that."
> **—Kristin Brumm, domestic violence awareness advocate**

QUESTION → RESPONSE   QUESTION → RESPONSE   QUESTION
↘ KEY ↗   ↘ KEY ↗
MESSAGE   MESSAGE

YOU IN CONTROL

By using some simple interview techniques, you can control the interview and make sure the target audience hears your story and key messages as you intend. Guiding and shaping the interview to best serve your advocacy goals requires you to practice deflecting/blocking, bridging, flagging, and headlining.

Deflecting/Blocking and Bridging

Sometimes a reporter's question can steer the interview to places you'd rather not go: to topics that don't relate to your story, uncomfortable areas, or information you'd rather not include in the interview. Certain statements by the reporter, too (such as an incorrect paraphrase of something you've said), might lead to misinformation, off-topic discussions, or an inappropriate frame to your story. To avoid this, you may need to *deflect* or *block* a question or statement, then *bridge* to a more desirable territory.

Bridging means moving smoothly from where the interview is to where you'd like it to go. Before you bridge, however, you may need to redirect a question or statement by deflecting it. At other times, you may need to completely block a statement before bridging back to your story or message. The objective is to respond and bridge quickly, so you don't give too much attention or weight to the question or statement you're deflecting or blocking. Here are some examples:

Deflect and bridge

– "That's a question a lot of people have, but what's really behind that question is…"

– "That's really the rare case. What we see much more often is…"

– "Rather than that, it's really a matter of access. Let me tell you the good news…"

Block and bridge

– "That's not my area of expertise, but what I *can* tell you is…"

– "I can't go into those kinds of details, but what I can tell about my experience…"

– "I don't see it that way. The way I see it is…"

Notice how, in these examples, the response does not repeat the incorrect or negative language the reporter may have used. Use nondescript pronouns or adjectives like *that* or *those kinds* rather than give currency to the reporter's phrasing.

Even when the interview's going well, you may need to bridge to your story or messages to ensure they're part of the interview. Again, don't wait for the right question to be asked. Bridge with simple statements, such as:

– "That's a great point. Another is…"

– "Let me just add…"

– "Let me put that into perspective…"

– "What I'm really here to talk about is…"

– "I think your audience would also be interested to know…"

– "That's another great example of how…"

> *Interviewer:* In terms of heart disease, your arteries are either clogged or they're not clogged, right? Is that right?
>
> *Kathy:* Well, no. There are different types of problems that can happen with your heart, and there are different types of heart disease you can have…
>
> —**Kathy Kastan, heart health advocate, blocking and bridging during a radio interview**

Flagging

Flagging is the verbal equivalent of using a highlighter to draw attention to the words and statements that will make reporters and audiences sit up and listen. When you "raise a flag," you'll hear the clacking of a computer keyboard on the other end of the call as the reporter makes notes. Your radio listeners will keep the car radio on after parking. Your television audiences will pause in their walks across the living room and stop in front of the screen to hear what you're saying.

By flagging, you let your audiences and the reporter know the most important points about the story and your messages. Try using some flagging words and phrases like these:

– "What's most important for people to understand…"

– "Here's why people need to hear this story…"

– "What we really want to make clear is…"

– "Here's what I think your listeners will be most interested in knowing…"

– "This is the most dangerous misconception people have…"

Headlining

Media interviews, whether print or broadcast, begin with the most important information at the top, followed by information that

> **Want a Great Headline?**
>
> Turn to Chapter Five, Craft Your Story, for tips on creating memorable hooks.

supports or explains. So provide the interviewer with a headline early in your interview, if not immediately. Headlining is absolutely critical in a broadcast interview. These interviews are typically quite brief, and you want to ensure that they'll highlight your key messages. Even in a print interview, headlining helps the reporter understand what the main theme of your story is; this process may even provide the actual headline for the written piece.

The next exercise, Bridge from Anywhere, was introduced to us by one of the advocates in our workshop.

If you're ready to practice for your upcoming interview, turn to the Seven Practice Runs in Chapter 9.

BRIDGE FROM ANYWHERE

Objective: *Practice getting from anywhere to your key messages and your story.*

Use this exercise to:
- Find natural links to your key messages
- Make bridges "second nature," not forced
- Amaze or amuse your family and friends

We once reconnected with an advocate who had been through our workshop a year or so earlier. She was a WomenHeart Champion, a woman with heart disease who was out speaking in her community and to the media, telling her story and delivering key educational messages about women and heart disease: Early detection. Accurate diagnosis. Proper treatment. She told us, "Thanks to you, I'm driving my family crazy."

"How so?" we asked.

She then told us how she practiced bridging at home.

I take whatever my family says to me and try to bridge back to my story or to the WomenHeart messages. For example, my husband's heading out to a meeting and he asks me whether there's gas in the car. I tell him that I noticed on the way home that the tank was low, so I stopped and filled it up. Then I bridge: ". . . which is yet another example of the importance of early detection, accurate diagnosis, and proper treatment . . ."

The Exercise
- Deftly bridge to your advocacy story and mission from a question a friend asks.

Chapter 9

Practice

IN THIS CHAPTER:

❏ Find out how speaking as an advocate is like performing jazz
❏ Learn healthy practice habits

Improvisational Speaking

On the continuum of speaking styles, *impromptu* lives on one end (speaking off-the-cuff with little or no preparation) and *manuscript speaking* is at the other (speaking from a script or teleprompter). Each style is appropriate at certain times. But when you're telling a personal story, these two styles are rarely desirable. You can't be totally impromptu or you'll risk presenting a raw, unprepared story; if you script it, you could come across as canned.

Somewhere between these two extremes is the style of speaking that enables you to be practiced, flexible, and natural. It's a style that requires you to decide key messages, how you'll tell your story, even specific wording you might use—even though what you say may come out differently each time you speak, as in natural conversation. It's a style that's adaptable to most situations, from informal talks to formal addresses

"I've never memorized anything word-for-word because, good grief, if you started getting off track, the rest of whatever you're trying to say is lost. So the most effective way that I've found is just to make bullet points and an outline. These are the points I want to talk about. And then just go from your heart— because people are going to take so much better to you and your message if they can tell that you're speaking from your heart and not from memorized words."

—**Loren Vaillancourt,**
advocate for stricter
distracted driving laws

to telephone interviews to on-camera appearances. Usually known as extemporaneous speaking, this style is more accurately called *improvisational*.

Not improvisational as in "creating something out of nothing," or "without preparation."

Improvisational like jazz.

A jazz musician playing "My Funny Valentine" knows the melody will always remain the same. Specific notes need to be hit each time it's played. But the musician improvises around the melody, playing it a bit differently each time, keeping the basic song structure yet bringing to it his or her unique voice, artistry, expression, and personality.

When you speak, you improvise around your story and key messages. What you say may change slightly or even dramatically each time, *but the tune remains the same*. Improvisational speaking, with its blend of preparation and spontaneity, enables you to speak naturally and focus attention where it should be: on your audience, on your story, on your messages and goals.

Jazz saxophonist Charlie Parker said it best: "You've got to learn your instrument. Then, you practice, practice, practice. And then, when you finally get up there on the bandstand, forget all that and just wail." This same philosophy applies to your preparation for advocacy. Speaking in public, whether you're interacting with an audience or a

"Back when I spoke in front of the President's Advisory Council on HIV/AIDS, I wanted to make sure I got my message across, so I had a script with me and my words in front of me. Nowadays, I will just put notes and bullet points down on my iPad or a couple of cue cards, and I'll go from there. I've gotten it pretty engrained, where I know what I want to say and I know what parts of my story I need to tell to have the biggest impact, based on the audience."

—Lawrence Stallworth II, HIV/AIDS awareness advocate

reporter, is a full-body experience involving your story, your voice, your body, your mind-set. The sooner you begin to practice *that* instrument, the more confident and clear you will be in the actual moment—when you "just wail."

Depending on your comfort level and experience, improvisational speaking may sound intimidating. Don't worry. Everything you do to prepare to tell your story as an advocate—choosing what to tell, focusing your story on your goals and messages, knowing who your audience is, and practicing—also prepares you to be more improvisational.

> "Don't script it. Tell your whole story to yourself, the entire thing, then find the parts that you really feel are important. Look at how much time you have and prioritize those points: these are the ones you hit, these are the ones you don't. Stick to that—and just tell it from your heart. Say, "This is what this means to me." Then everything else will follow. Say it with feeling. And don't fake it."
>
> **—Derek Cotton, advocate for cancer support services**

Part of the unease some feel in embracing improvisational speaking comes from a strong desire for perfection, a feeling that if a word doesn't come out quite right or a phrase is forgotten, you've blown the whole presentation or interview. Rarely is this the case. An audience is not aware of the perfection in your head. They only know the communication that's happening between you and them, in the moment. Aim for connection, not perfection. As saxophonist Coleman Hawkins said about making music, "If you don't make mistakes, you're not really trying." Accept that there may be imperfections; correct them when necessary and move on. It's worth it to get to the more natural and conversational style that is improvisational speaking.

Good Practice Habits

Ultimately, you'll find the practice methods that work best for you. But here are some guiding principles to keep in mind as you find your own routine.

Define Your Individual Style

Ask a roomful of people to describe how they'd like to be viewed as advocates, and chances are you'll hear a lot of similar responses: clear, confident, effective, engaging. But keep asking, and you'll start to hear how differently people describe their individual styles: one person wants to be perceived as warm, another as forceful. One hopes to come across as precise, another as energizing. As you prepare and practice your advocacy skills, think about how you want people to describe *you* as an advocate. What is *your* individual style and voice? Use these tips to find out.

- **Ask.** Get into the habit of asking your peers and partners for honest assessments of your effectiveness and whether you're coming across as you'd like.
- **Challenge.** Be as clear about how you *don't* want to be perceived as you are how you *do* want to be perceived.
- **Gut-check.** Most of us know when something feels artificial. Listen to your gut. If the words or expressions you're using feel forced, ask whether you're speaking naturally or imitating someone else's style.

Once you've determined what your individual style is and how it may be coming across to others, these tips will help you stay on track:

- **Write it down.** Keep a written description of what you want your individual style to be. Refer to it as you practice.
- **Assess.** Use your written description as the gauge for measuring your progress. When you watch or listen to your recorded practice or appearance, ask: What am I doing that creates the style I want? What am I doing that detracts from it?

Internalize Your Structure

The more you tell your stories as an advocate, the more likely you are to repeat some phrases, sentences, and even paragraphs. After all, you've crafted certain language specifically to engage your audiences, and you've composed a few excellent headlines to hook them. But it's doubtful you'll ever memorize an entire story, presentation, or interview appearance word for word.

When speaking improvisationally, though, you have in mind a basic structure, a road map, that remains fixed regardless of the particular presentation or interview you're giving. Just as a jazz musician sets the notes of the song and chords to memory to guide improvisation, you can aim to *internalize the basic structure* of your story, presentation, or interview. That structure might be the arrangement of the pieces of your experience; an outline of your talk's intro, body, and conclusion; or the key messages that guide your interview responses. Use these pointers to work on internalizing your structure:

- **Map it.** Use your Story Map or sketch a skeletal outline to set the structure in your visual memory.

- **Practice aloud.** Vocalizing and moving or gesturing as you practice helps "set it in the body."
- **Visualize.** Do a mental run-through of your talk or interview as you sit calmly or as you fall asleep.
- **U.A.M.D.** That means "Use A Mnemonic Device." Come up with a clever memory aid like spelling a short word with the initial letters of your key messages.
- **Talk structure.** Use the Practice Run on page 174, "Talk the Structure," and try speaking *just* the organization of your talk: "I'll start off talking about my trip to Italy. I'll preview my presentation with…then I'll hit my first key message… then I'll transition to my second key message…"

Harness the Butterflies

We've all felt nervousness and know how disconcerting it can be. However, don't try to eliminate your nervous energy. You want to channel this surge of adrenaline in a productive way. Think of it as a personal reservoir of extra energy you need to bring passion to your advocacy and to stay focused. Your goal is to learn to tap that reservoir.

Harnessing the butterflies you may feel before speaking is not something that happens with a flick of a switch. It comes with practice and experience, and all the preparation outlined in *Living Proof* is aimed at increasing your confidence and comfort so you can channel your energy. Here are some additional reminders:

- **Practice aloud.** Have we stressed this enough? It's the only way to get your body, voice, and mind ready. For presentations, it's how you clock your time; for interviews, it's how you practice responses to potential questions.

- **Be realistic.** You don't have to be perfect. Remember that audiences and interviewers are generally supportive and forgiving.
- **Use relaxation techniques.** Breathe deeply. Shake out your hands and arms. Roll your shoulders. Roll your head. Reduce the tension in your throat by yawning and humming.
- **Be healthy.** Get lots of rest and drink plenty of water the day you are to speak. Speaking publicly is a physically engaging activity. Train for it.
- **Use video recordings whenever possible.** Okay, it may be a little painful at first to watch yourself practicing your presentation or being interviewed, but video recording is an invaluable addition to your preparation. It's most useful for becoming aware of things you *don't* think about when speaking: word choice; repetitive phrases, gestures, or stances; eye contact; clothing that distracts. If you really want to see whether you pace too much or have an unconscious nervous gesture, play the video in fast motion and watch how often you repeat various motions. The only way to know how you look on-camera is to be on-camera.

EXERCISE

SEVEN PRACTICE RUNS

Objective: Approach your practice from a variety of directions.

Use this exercise to:
- Get ready for specific talks or interviews
- Become more improvisational
- Generate content and language
- Guard against a "canned" and over-rehearsed style

Throughout *Living Proof*, we talk about your preparation for advocacy as practice rather than rehearsal. Rehearsal typically implies a trial performance that approximates the situation as fully as possible: you're in the environment, wearing what you'll wear, using your full voice and energy and running it from start to finish, perhaps before an audience. While it's certainly possible you may need that kind of rehearsal for an event or appearance, most of the speaking or interview situations you prepare for probably require a more improvisational style. For that reason, we recommend preparing yourself through practice runs.

The following Practice Runs ask you to approach your preparation in a variety of ways.

The Exercise

The more ways you practice your story, the more improvisational and confident you will be. For all of these practice runs, record and make notes of your insights or work with a partner.

Practice Run 1: What You Need to Know
- Imagine your audience before you. Sit or stand comfortably, set a timer for 3 minutes, and start speaking. The theme of this free-telling is "Why it's important for you to hear my experience."
- Keep talking for the full 3 minutes. Use one of these phrases to begin, and return to it if you get stuck:
  - "It's important for you to hear my experience because . . ."
  - "Here's how my experience relates to you . . ."
  - "I think you may be surprised to know this about my experience . . ."

SEVEN PRACTICE RUNS (*continued*)

Practice Run 2: Speak the Start
- If preparing for a presentation, practice just the first 30 seconds. Practice sitting or standing as you will at the start. Think about what happens right before you speak. Concentrate on starting strong.
- If preparing for an interview, practice your very first answer. Imagine the interviewer asks you an open-ended question: "What happened?"

Practice Run 3: Speak the Finish
- If preparing for a presentation, practice just the last 30 seconds. Practice sitting or standing as you will at the end of your talk. Think about what happens right afterward. Concentrate on ending strong.
- If preparing for an interview, practice your last answer. Imagine the interviewer says, "We only have 30 seconds left. Is there anything else you want our audience to know?"

Practice Run 4: Talk the Structure
- Focus on the structure of your story or presentation, or the key messages you will stress in your interview. Practice speaking the structure, for example:
  - "I begin with the startling statistic, then explain why I'm here today. I preview my key messages, then transition to my story..."
  - "The three key messages I'm going to return to in the interview are...."

Practice Run 5: Tarzan-ing
- Think about how you've chosen to tell your story and the order in which you'll tell events or episodes. Focus on the *transitions* between moments or events. Practice just the transitions (like Tarzan, swinging from vine to vine).
- If preparing for a talk or presentation, think of the structure. Focus on the transitions between intro, body, and conclusion and practice just those transitions.
- If preparing for an interview, use the Bridge from Anywhere exercise on page 163.
- This is a particularly useful practice run if you're working with visual aids. Practice just the transitions from visual to visual.

SEVEN PRACTICE RUNS (*continued*)

Practice Run 6: Soft Ball
- If preparing for an interview, write a list of questions you're hoping the reporter will ask you. Make them open-ended questions ("What happened?") or directly related to your advocacy goal ("Why is this important?" "What do you want people to do?").
- Have a partner ask you the questions, or make an audio-recording of them and practice responding while alone. Practice multiple responses.

Practice Run 7: Hard Ball
- If preparing for an interview, write a list of questions you're hoping the reporter doesn't ask you. Look at Chapter 14, "Handling Questions from an Interviewer" (page 260), where we've included common types of challenging questions and effective answers. Think of questions that would take the interview in the wrong direction or directly challenge your advocacy.
- Have a partner ask you the questions, or make an audio-recording of the questions and practice responding while alone. Practice multiple responses.

Chapter 10

Where Stories Lead

IN THIS CHAPTER:

- ❏ Stepping forward and making a difference
- ❏ Preparing to be surprised
- ❏ Keeping your focus where it should be

Stepping Forward, Making a Difference

The reasons advocates go public with personal experiences are as varied as the stories they tell. So, too, are the places advocacy takes them.

Like Kathy Kastan, you may have found your original motivation in the desire to feel you're giving back. She began as a spokeswoman for the organization that helped her find proper treatment for heart disease. Now she has a new career as an advocate and educator.

Like Theresa Greenleaf, mom of a child with allergies, you might first share your story under specific circumstances such as a grade school parent's meeting. Someone may have seen the potential in your story even before you did, as when cancer survivor Derek Cotton was asked to help advocate for a cancer support organization.

Like Gayathri Ramprasad, LeDerick Horne, or Carey Christensen, you may be taking an adversity like depression, a learning disability, or a disease and turning it into powerful inspiration and advocacy for others, contributing to the efforts of a large initiative or sponsor, or even founding your own organization. You may be in a leadership position like Scott Harrison, Teresa Opheim, or Ocean Robbins, linking your story to your organization's mission as they do when they advocate for clean drinking water, sustainable agriculture, or environmental stewardship.

A life-altering event may propel you now to speak to the media, to large online audiences, or to small groups in high school gymnasiums—as Loren Vaillancourt does when advocating for stricter distracted driving laws or when Kristin Brumm tells her story of domestic violence. Or, like Becky Blanton, Lawrence Stallworth II, or Zach Wahls, your story may land you on the world stage.

Becky had the rare opportunity to first tell her story of homelessness at the TED Global Conference:

> It felt scary. It felt exciting. It felt lonely. It felt sad. It felt liberating. I cycled through each of those emotions over and over. I remember thinking, "If I do this, there's no going back."

You can view a video of her presentation at TED.com (www.ted.com)—which means Becky's story now reaches an enormous audience. She's heard from scores of others who have found themselves in similar circumstances, and her hopeful message that "we are not defined by where we live" has touched many.

Her presentation has also rubbed people the wrong way. Since entering the complex conversation about homelessness via the platform afforded her by TED.com, Becky has also heard criticism about everything from the details of her story to not properly framing the issue to the presentation itself.

When the video of the speech made by Zach Wahls to the Iowa House of Representatives went viral, his story—an Eagle Scout with two moms—spread rapidly. He was thrust into the limelight and appeared on talk shows of David Letterman, Jon Stewart, and Ellen DeGeneres. He says, "I, the medium, became the message, a message that resonated both among those who

support the advancement of LGBT rights and those who do not."[1]
He was attacked in the media by bloggers and talk-radio hosts
who took his speech apart word by word, dismissed it as merely
"argument from anecdote," and leveled personal assaults on
his character.

Becky and Zach's experiences are important reminders that
there is always some risk when you step forward—and how
important it is to stay focused on your goals. Becky advises:

Anyone who tells their story has to realize that people may
criticize. You have to come to terms with that and be strong
in who you are. Having a support system in place is really
helpful. Focus on the positive. Revisit your motives.

Zach likewise stresses the importance of building a network to
support you in your public advocacy:

I needed to build a really good community around me, which
includes family and friends and coworkers and people who
share my world views—but also who challenge my world
views. Having a good ecosystem of people around you
and in place to have those conversations is really important.

And it's not only when you are challenged that it's important
to maintain focus; it's just as important when you are successful in
your advocacy, when you deliver a lot of powerful presentations
and give countless great interviews. As the value of your story is
recognized, you may be called upon to speak more frequently, and
you may attain a measure of local or national recognition. You
may even find that "advocate" becomes your main public persona,

and you are a frequent subject of media attention. If you are fortunate to achieve this level of interest, heed the advice of other sought-after advocates and spokespersons: always remember why you chose to speak out. Keep that reason at the core of your advocacy and the focus will stay where it should be: on the positive change and the difference you want to make. Enjoy the increasingly larger platforms and audiences that your story and your advocacy have gained.

Since speaking publicly in local high schools about his HIV-positive status only a few months after his diagnosis at age seventeen, Lawrence Stallworth II has spoken at the United Nations, at the United States Conference on AIDS, and now— at twenty-three—is the youngest member of the Presidential Advisory Council on HIV/AIDS. About his advocacy journey, Lawrence says:

> How many people are in my shoes? How many 23-year olds get to say, "I'm advising the President of the United States of America?" Had you told me six years ago that I would be the new face of young black people living with HIV and AIDS, I would have said you were crazy.

Still, Lawrence remains focused on his advocacy goal:

> This is a great thing for me…but it's also not about me. It's about helping my community and people who are living with HIV and AIDS. I see it as another platform, one where I get to make recommendations that will affect people's lives. Fate has a way of putting you where you need to be.

Our final bit of advice comes from a sentiment we hear expressed by many advocates who've been out speaking and giving interviews, some for many years: be prepared to be surprised by the impact you're really making. No matter how much anyone prepares you for the potential your story has to make a difference, you can't know how it will actually happen...until it happens. And this is important to remember, because it's easy to lose steam or worry whether the story of one person really, truly, can have an impact.

For LeDerick Horne, a reminder came from a young man named Carlos who approached him after a presentation LeDerick had delivered at a Youth Leadership Summit. Like LeDerick, Carlos had a learning disability but had persevered through high school as well as college and now was advocating for others. He said:

> "It's so easy, especially for people who are passionate about making a difference in the world, to just work and work and work yourself. But being able to set time aside and go through a process of personal restoration, whatever that looks like, that's very, very important."
> **—Zach Wahls**

LeDerick, the reason I'm at this summit is because I heard you speak when I was in high school. I don't know if you know this, but I was homeless then. And hearing you let me know I'd be able to go to college. Man, you had no idea. I needed to hear your message at that moment. I needed to hear you to keep me going and to let me know there was more for me after high school.

For mental health advocate Gayathri Ramprasad, it was a young woman who approached her after a speech to say "Tonight was going to be the night. I had decided I was going to end it all tonight. But listening to your story…"

Carey Christensen, who sits on the patient advisory board for the Michael J. Fox Foundation, is reminded of the changes she's seen since first speaking out—and the continuing responsibility she feels:

> "I try to really savor those moments. When you step off-stage and you're headed to the next workshop, or trying to get to the airport, there might be a student who walks up to you and says, 'hey that was really great,' and stops you to shake your hand. That's a big deal."
> —LeDerick Horne, advocate for people with learning disabilities

There have been some real changes in the political landscape and in research concerning Parkinson's. I feel like, for a long time, I was just a voice in the wilderness saying, "Somebody pay attention." Now, people are paying attention.

When I'm flying from my home near Seattle to a meeting in New York and I'm flying over the U.S., I think of all the people that I have flown over and ask, "How many of them have Parkinson's?" Then I get into the subway or the train at JFK and I go into Manhattan. And going through these neighborhoods with all these people in them, I think, "How many of them have Parkinson's?" But I am the one that gets to go sit at a conference table at the Michael J. Fox Foundation; I feel a big responsibility as a person with Parkinson's. I mean, I owe it to them to do a good job, to speak the truth even when it is hard.

Finally, reflecting on his long experience as a public advocate—which started when he was a teen—Ocean Robbins is impressed by the many places personal stories have taken him.

I have learned through the years how deeply people respond to authenticity and deep humanity. It resonates and pulls them in. Sometimes, our most painful and traumatic moments carry within them the gift of a deeply moving story that resonates with very deep places in our audience. I knew there must be a way to leverage my family story to bring attention to causes I cherished. In time, I learned that telling my story could also open doorways of contact with people who identified as wealthy and famous, with social justice activists, with parents, grandparents, and children. In short, it could be a doorway of connection with almost everyone.

We wish you the best in making a difference in your world and encountering the surprises along the way.

Part
TWO

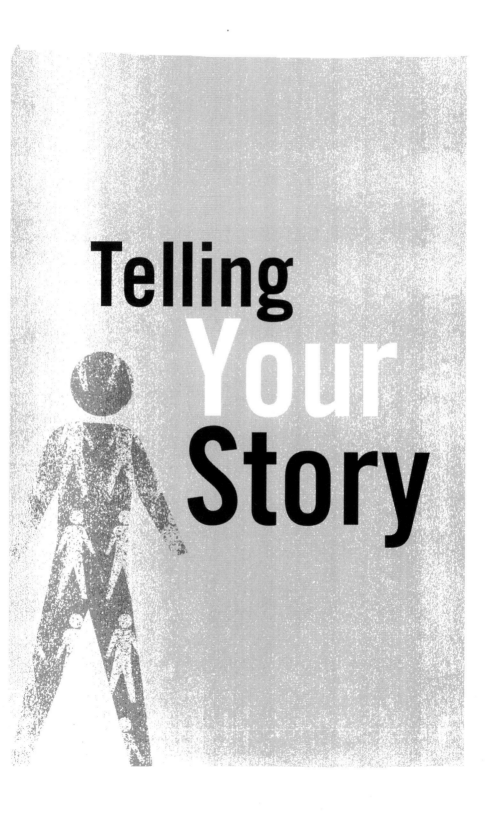

Telling Your Story

Chapter 11

Moving from Silence to Story

IN THIS CHAPTER:

❏ Exploring the space between private and public spheres
❏ Making considered choices about speaking out
❏ Addressing the barriers advocates often run up against

Standing at the Threshold

Making the decision to share your personal stories as an advocate places you at the threshold between the private and the public. Over the years, we've heard advocates describe their "threshold moments" in many ways: as times of great uncertainty or exhilarating potential, as periods of intense reflection or powerful determination. How is it for you?

Perhaps, like many advocates, you step across that threshold easily; your decision to speak is straightforward and natural, even inevitable. You may sense some amount of risk or uncertainty in going public, but for you, that risk is minimal compared to your commitment to tell your story and make a difference. Or perhaps, like other advocates, you find the space between the private and the public an unsettling one, where you encounter feelings about what is and is not appropriate to share, what makes a "good" story or what is at stake by speaking out. Though your motivation to be an advocate is strong, you wonder about certain challenges that may lie ahead.

There can be a lot going on in the space between the private and the public, and how you experience moving through this transition is as unique and personal as your reasons for speaking out.

The experience of moving from private to public is what psychologists and anthropologists might call liminal: being betwixt and between. (The word *liminal* is from the Latin for "threshold.") Examples of liminal experiences include life changes and rites of passage like graduation, divorce, bar mitzvah, or joining a new community or culture. In periods of liminality, we're aware that we are becoming someone else. As you become a public advocate, you're stepping into a new identity, surely. But this liminal moment also may have a deeper significance for your sense of identity as you find your voice or discover new purpose.

Paul Loeb, writing about the choice to be socially involved in *Soul of a Citizen*,[1] captures this sense of standing on the brink— and the rewards that come with stepping forward:

> Rarely does social involvement place us in the path of destructive natural forces or armed opponents, but it does involve risk. At the very least, it requires us to make ourselves psychologically vulnerable. It impels us to overcome distracting habits and petty concerns, to challenge internal fears, and to face criticism from those who call our efforts fruitless, foolish, or a waste of scarce time.
>
> In return, social involvement converts us from detached spectators into active participants. We develop new competencies and strengths. We form strong bonds with coworkers of courage and vision. Our lives become charged with purpose.

Standing on the threshold between the private and the public, however, you may encounter a swirl of conflicting feelings that challenge whether you *should* step forward: What is and is not appropriate to share? Am I entitled to speak? What will others think of me? What constitutes a "story worth telling?" If you've encountered some of these challenging thoughts or feelings, you're not alone. Here are four areas where advocates sometimes bump up against barriers to going public.

Navigating Emotions

I f the life experiences you plan to share as an advocate are charged with intimate emotions, you may wonder: "How personal or candid should I be?" and "How personal or candid am I comfortable being?" Your answers depend on many things,

> "You will know when it is time to tell the story, you will also know when it is not time. Some experiences need more gestation time than others. Listen to yourself."[2]
> —Tami Spry

such as how close you are to experiences—both psychologically and in time—and how often you've spoken about them. Your answers may also depend on how the people closest to you might react to what you have to say. Decisions about personal disclosure are different for everyone.

The Five Qualities of the Well-Told Advocacy Story help you navigate this terrain. For example, Loren Vaillancourt, an advocate for distracted driving laws, points to the importance of *focus* and *practice* when telling the difficult story of her brother's death in a car crash:

Telling my brother's story and saying what happened, it's really emotionally overwhelming. I was not able to get through my story at first. There was no way. It took practice. I had to talk it through to myself. I had to take a moment, find a way to get myself out and realize what's important. It's about being able to ask, "What is the point of this story?" And honestly, if you practice it, it helps you with that [emotional] transition: "I'm trying to get my point across here so, okay, where do I need to go next?"

If the emotional content of your experience is something you're wrestling with as you choose what to tell, keep these tips in mind.

- **Know your boundaries, but don't omit the heart.** Sometimes you have to step outside yourself to look at your story objectively. At other times, you have to dive deeply into it. Your goal is neither to distance yourself from emotions nor to bare your soul in the name of full disclosure. Your aim is a balanced and effective telling—neither raw nor canned—that is emotionally engaging, not fragile or distanced.
- **You are the author of your experience.** The decision to disclose or not is *always* yours. Never leave that decision to chance or to others—for instance, to a reporter or audience member who asks an inappropriately personal question.
- **Remember your goal and your audience.** Ask: What is required of this moment, this audience, at this event or interview? What you decide to share may be appropriate for some audiences but inappropriate for others. Knowing your audience is vital. Some audiences will require bold and graphic honesty, while others may require a gentler, more measured approach.

For suggestions on how to manage emotions that come up during the actual telling of your story, look to Chapter 13, Public Speaking: Tips and Tools. Again, paying attention to the five qualities of the well-told advocacy story (see Chapter 1) as you prepare will help you find the balance between raw and canned storytelling.

Addressing the Cultural Censors

P art of the journey from silence to story involves uncovering and understanding the potential of your story to be a powerful tool of advocacy. That potential isn't always immediately self-evident and, as facilitators and coaches of new advocates, we often begin by helping advocates find the connections between their lived experiences and the difference they want to make in the world. Before people find those connections, it's not uncommon to hear them dismiss their stories out of hand: "I don't really have a story," or "My story's not the important one," or "I shouldn't talk about…" Why does this initial impulse to hold back stories often appear in the space between private and public? It may be the cultural censors at work.

Most of us carry notions of what personal stories are or are not appropriate to share publicly. The messages we've received throughout our lives—from family, community, society, institutions, and the media—shape our views of which stories are relevant, whose stories are privileged. Some of those messages were "personally delivered" in our formative years, in the intimate webs of our families and communities of origin, where speaking out was either encouraged or discouraged. If the messages you received were positive and affirming, you probably now feel secure in the value of your story. If, however, you heard negative and stifling messages, they may still echo within you and challenge your decision to step forward and tell your stories.

The space between the private and the public is the nexus of the personal and the social, if not political. It's where we meet the strong or subtle cultural censors who attempt to define what community, race, class, or gender can or cannot speak, to tell us which stories are told and valued and which are not. In short, it's where we're reminded of the power of personal stories and the power of the storyteller. As the Ewe-Mina proverb goes, "Until lions have their own storytellers, tales of the hunt shall always glorify the hunter."

> When stories are told over and over and become accepted as "the way things are," they become *dominant narratives*. Dominant narratives help maintain existing power structures. But *counter narratives* constantly challenge the dominant, offering alternative stories that challenge "what is true."

When negative messages from the cultural censors become internalized, they contribute to our personal sense of worth, agency or "permission to speak." As you consider telling your story as an advocate, you may need to challenge the messages you've received and to ask: where are these messages coming from—and will I choose to heed them? Becoming a vocal advocate often requires you to identify what keeps you from speaking out.

- **Revisit the rules you grew up with**, rules about who gets to speak or who gets to speak first.
- **Examine old communication norms** that were based on your age, status, or gender.
- **Reflect on a learned communication style** that either favored or disapproved of personal disclosure.

For many advocates, sharing their stories publicly is a direct and strategic challenge to the power of cultural censorship. Mental health and lung cancer advocates, for example, use their personal stories to confront societal stigmas of shame, blame,

and stereotype assigned to an illness—stigma they may have felt
personally as they stood at the threshold.

When Gayathri Ramprasad was in the midst of her MBA
program, she decided to fulfill an assignment in her Effective
Communications class by focusing on a favorite quote that
had helped see her through her recovery from mental illness:
"Courage is fear that has said its prayers." To talk about this
quote in her speech, however, she would have to come out to her
classmates as someone who had experienced mental illness; she
had never spoken publicly about this before. While supported
and encouraged by her professor, Gayathri knew this first public
admission still placed her firmly on the threshold of the private
and the public, where she heard the swirl of voices, many arising
from cultural and societal pressures:

> First, there was the fear of disclosure that keeps most people
> struggling with mental illness silent and isolated. Will I be
> embraced as the same student that I had been all through
> these years? Will I be treated differently? Will I be judged
> differently? Or does this truth of mine completely change our
> relationship and my future in this program? And then, coming
> from the Indian culture where safeguarding my family's honor
> is my duty; outing myself, letting the world know that there
> is mental illness in my family, would be a huge black mark—
> or so we have been told to perceive it. I was embracing an
> identity that has long been stigmatized.
>
> Still, I was born and raised in a country where the phrase
> on all of our flags and our currency is *Satyameva Jayate*: truth
> alone triumphs.
>
> We are only as sick as the secrets we keep.

Whether it is fighting stigma, going against what you've been told is "appropriate," or asserting the power of your voice to be part of a larger conversation, you may find that telling your stories has a deeply personal and political significance.

Avoiding "The Story Game"

We once sat in a room with an inspiring group of advocates for WomenHeart: The National Coalition for Women with Heart Disease. All had suffered some form of cardiovascular trouble—congenital heart disease, heart failure, or multiple heart attacks. Their stories were amazing. Every one of them provided living proof of why we need to pay attention to heart disease in women. Each woman shared her story with the group, and when it was Helene's turn, she began, "Well, my story isn't very dramatic. I only had the one heart attack."

We think about that moment often, especially when we hear new advocates express some variation of Helene's comment: "My story isn't very interesting," or "There's really not much of a story here," or "There are better stories people should hear." In other words: "My story doesn't measure up."

Why does this tendency toward self-deprecation appear in the space between private and public? Sometimes it's the cultural censors at work again; at other times, it's what we call "getting caught in the Story Game." Getting caught in the Story Game is a trap that's easy to fall into because it's built on something we're all aware of, on some level: stories are in competition.

The Story Game is played out around us constantly: entertainment and news stories fight for audiences, business brand stories vie for our dollars and consumer loyalty, and faith narratives compete for our beliefs and behaviors. In today's business world, the Story Game can get pretty intense. An arsenal of books with titles like *Winning the Story Wars*, *Whoever Tells the Best Story Wins*, and *Jab, Jab, Jab, Right Hook* arms players with tools to make sure their stories are competition ready. Nonprofit

> **The power of your story may not lie in its drama, but in its absolutely perfect relationship to your cause.**

organizations and cause marketing campaigns, too, rely on individuals' personal stories—perhaps yours—to engage audiences in meaningful ways and compete for mindshare and dollars. And as already noted, the fierce competition of cultural narratives is often at the base of power struggles.

But here's the danger of an *individual* advocate getting caught in the Story Game trap: he or she may assume that if stories are in competition, then *life experiences* must also be in competition. In other words, we sometimes assume certain kinds of life experiences make better advocacy stories: those that are the *most* dramatic, *most* emotional, *most* ... fill in the blank. While it's true the events of one person's life may seem more sensational than another's, this doesn't discount individual experience. The power of your story may not lie in its drama, but in its absolutely perfect relationship to your cause. *A "good" advocacy story is one that provides living proof of your advocacy message—pure and simple.*

Kristin Brumm's story of surviving domestic violence is powerful living proof; so is Teresa Opheim's story of watching her grandparents' farm gradually disappear. Our lives unfold in many ways, and our stories can be told in many ways. Whether your story charts a journey from adversity to advocacy or focuses on quiet moments packed with significance—your story has value if it contributes to your advocacy and connects with your audience.

When we get caught in the Story Game, we ignore what successful advocacy groups confirm: advocacy needs personal stories of *all* kinds. Audiences vary, and what engages them will change. Advocacy needs stories that move large audiences—incredible stories of overcoming adversity, fighting horrible injustice, or emerging from extraordinary circumstances. But advocacy also needs "small" stories—a moment witnessed, a statement overheard, an insight gained. Advocacy needs stories that are told at rallies and across kitchen tables, in the national media and on front doorsteps.

In this arena, where we use personal stories for advocacy, "winning" is not determined by a particular type of story or a particular kind of life experience. As advocates, we judge the value of personal stories by their ability to support a message

> "Every place we save has its story. Every place we conserve has its relationships and its connections: the story of a vacant, rubble-strewn lot in Central Harlem that the spirit of one woman and her love for her father turn into an urban oasis of hope and community spirit; the story of homecoming, healing, and restitution as a Native American tribe returns after more than a century to its ancestral homeland..., the story of a child's personal discovery and wonder at play in a forest or irrigation ditch that is later threatened with development. In our work we are surrounded by stories about hope, stories about healing, stories about fairness, stories about making a difference, stories about community, stories about connection."[3]
>
> **—Will Rogers, president, Trust for Public Land**

and affect an audience. They don't need to affect *every* audience, just *an* audience. Whether your story has the potential to move millions or a roomful of people, it is worth exploring as a tool of advocacy.

Choosing Safety

Standing on the threshold between private and public, you may find yourself debating internally whether you should speak. This internal debate deserves attention: It may be about protection.

Kristin Brumm had started her blog, Wanderlust, in 2009 to share stories of her affinity for travel and her day-to-day musings. When she and her husband began divorce proceedings later that year, she was open with her readers about the process and how she was feeling. But in 2010, in the midst of the divorce, she found herself a victim of domestic violence. She entered a state of fear that worsened after she discovered her ex-husband was in possession of child pornography and had several weapons hidden around her house. After the violence, she found herself hesitant and silent, uncertain whether and how to share her story.

> I hadn't talked much on my blog about what was really happening. I'd held off for fear of retaliation, either litigative or physical. Such is the dynamic of abuse: "Don't speak or else." So for the longest time I was afraid to speak.

Ultimately, however, Kristin reached a point at which she weighed her desire to speak against the threats she faced:

I was tired of running and I was tired of sitting in silence. And when so much had already been lost, the risk of speaking out took on a slighter weight. I made the decision to speak because I felt I was already in about as much danger as I could be in. And I thought maybe if I shine a spotlight on this danger that that would somehow help.

You are *always* the author of your stories. Ultimately, you are responsible for deciding what is appropriate to share publicly and what risks you're willing to assume by sharing. That may mean taking into account very real matters of safety. When physical and psychological safety is at stake, it may be wise and necessary *not* to go public—at least not here and not now. As facilitators and trainers, we often must support someone's choice *not* to tell a story as much as we encourage others to do so.

- If your story is too raw, you may need emotional protection until you feel strong enough to share it (see "Navigating Emotions," page 192).
- When stories arise from violence or abuse, physical safety may remain a threat and must take precedence. Seek counsel from trusted agencies or authorities, crisis centers, safe spaces, or faith communities.
- If telling your story could have ramifications for those around you, consider their well-being. This suggestion applies not only to legal implications if proceedings are in process but also to the possibility that sharing your story may put others at risk. Remember, too, that stories that arise from violence, abuse, or other trauma may contain "triggers" for listeners who may have suffered, and are still dealing with, their own trauma.

In Kristin's case, coming forward with her story helped with the eventual prosecution and sentencing of her ex-husband. Since then, sharing her story has led her further into advocacy and she currently is executive vice president of a domestic violence services agency.

When I first began telling my story of living with abuse and coming to terms with my ex-husband's crimes, I didn't do it to change anyone else's life. I did it so that I could connect with others in a time of need, and also to try to make sense of what I was going through. However, as the situation progressed, I realized that my story could make a difference in the lives of others as well. I was able to use it to advocate for other victims of domestic violence. And then when I started telling it, women, but also some men, began contacting me saying, "Thank you, this is my experience, too."

As you cross the threshold as an advocate from private to public, from silence to story, you will discover your power; you may also confront yourself. But, whether your journey across the threshold is smooth or halted, it's worthwhile pausing and exploring what you encounter in the space between the private and the public.

Chapter 12

Public Speech, Public Narrative

Personal Stories and Persuasion

What does it mean to be an advocate?

In its broadest sense, *advocacy* means "any public action to support and recommend a cause, policy or practice." That covers a lot of public actions, from displaying a bumper sticker to sounding off with a bullhorn. But whether the action is slapping something on the back of a car or speaking in front of millions, every act of advocacy involves making some kind of public statement, one that says, "I support this." Advocacy is a communicative act.

Advocacy is also a persuasive act. "I support this" is usually followed by another statement (sometimes only implied): "...and you should, too." Advocacy not only means endorsing a cause or idea, but recommending, promoting, defending, or arguing for it. The word *advocate* has its origins in ancient Roman law; the *advocatus* was the legal counsel who pleaded cases in the court of justice, "a gifted speaker who could elevate his defense to an intellectual, philosophical and rhetorical level."[1] One of the most noted *advocati* was Cicero, famed Roman lawyer and politician. Advocacy is, at its root, spoken persuasive communication.

But there's an important nuance to the meaning of advocacy, one that informs much of *Living Proof*. The Latin root of advocate, *ad vocare*, means "to be called." Cicero and other *advocati* were summoned to court to plead cases *on behalf of others*. Roman citizens outside the court also used the word *advocatus* to mean "any person who gave another his aid in any business, as a witness, for instance."[2]

This more complete, altruistic definition of advocacy—spoken persuasive communication on behalf of or to the benefit of others—is one we kept in the forefront as we wrote *Living Proof.*

The question at the heart of *Living Proof* is this: When does a personal story work as a persuasive tool of advocacy—and when does it not? Having worked with thousands of advocates and hundreds of organizations over the past twenty years, we believe the answer to that question very often has less to do with *what* the story is and more with *how* and *why* it's told: how the speaker relates the story to the advocacy goal and the audience, and why the speaker is advocating. The most successful public advocates have found a unique mind-set and disposition toward their public acts of advocacy. Even though the contexts of their advocacy can vary widely—from urging new legislation to fighting discrimination to raising awareness of an issue to inspiring action and behavioral change to raising money for a cause—they all share a similar rhetorical stance.

Rhetorical stance refers to a speaker's role or behavior in relation to the subject, to the audience, and to his or her own persona (or character).[3] Advocates who are most successful advocating with their personal stories adopt a rhetorical stance that has these traits:

- **The subject** is the advocacy goal, one that is necessary, attainable, pointed toward positive change, and benefiting a greater good.
- **The audience** is comprised of those who will benefit from achieving the goal, whether as direct recipients (of

better health, of happier lives, of justice, etc.) or as allies in advancing positive change.

- **The speaker's persona or character** is that of one who speaks in order to benefit others or to share benefits with others.

This last aspect—the speaker's persona or character—is sometimes the most challenging for advocates to navigate when using their personal stories as persuasive proof. Advocacy is, by its nature, focused on the benefit to others; it is audience-centered (Chapter 7, page 126). Yet, featuring the speaker's personal story can give the impression that it's the speaker who is in the spotlight. The most successful advocates learn how to negotiate their personae, keeping focus on the advocacy goal and its benefit to others.

> "I know that my story is the power, but ultimately it is not about me. It's about what my story can do for others. There is no point in telling it otherwise."
> —**Carey Christensen, advocate for Parkinson's research**

This is why many of our recommendations in *Living Proof* aim at helping speakers achieve a balance "between personal story and public good." For example, a "raw" telling of a personal story (page 28), one in which the speaker is unfocused, emotionally fragile, or unbridled, can make the communicative act seem to be about the speaker rather than the advocacy goal. A slick, sensationalized, "canned" telling of a personal story can do the

> "Our storytelling work here is an effort to tell a story that involves the head and the heart AND moves people to use their hands and feet in action."[4]
> —**350.org**

same, leading the audience to focus on and perhaps scrutinize the speaker's intent, rather than engage with the message. The "Five Qualities of the Well-Told Advocacy Story" (Chapter 1, page 33) and additional recommendations throughout *Living Proof* help speakers situate themselves between the raw and canned extremes, where they can tell their personal stories effectively while concentrating on their ultimate goal: making a positive difference for the audience or creating a positive condition that speaker and audience can share.[5]

More than 2300 years ago, Aristotle defined the essential elements of persuasion: *ethos*, *logos*, and *pathos*. These three types of persuasive appeals are the building blocks for creating communication that will move an audience to accept a message or take a desired action. In the simplest terms, these appeals can be described as follows:

- **Ethos.** Appeals that develop the character of the speaker
- **Logos.** Appeals that use logic and reason
- **Pathos.** Appeals that engage or activate the audience's emotions or imagination

Telling stories—not just personal stories, but all forms of narrative—is one of the most common ways speakers employ pathos and awaken emotions in an audience. Whether true-to-life or fictional, told across a kitchen table or on the big screen, stories have the power to make us smile, laugh, cry, or fume.

> "Stories are commonly thought of both as authentic and as deceptive ("telling my story" versus "telling stories"). They are seen as universal in their implications and as dangerously particularistic—idiosyncratic, even. Storytelling is appreciated, enjoyed, and distrusted."[6]
>
> **—Francesca Polletta**

But stories do more than simply elicit emotional responses—and pathos is more than simply "playing on emotions." Stories also engage our imaginations through things like evocative language, sensory imagery, and metaphor. Stories make abstract concepts concrete and understandable, as in Hans Roslings' popular TED talks (https://www.ted.com/speaker/hans_rosling), in which the global health expert makes statistics come to life, narrating their movements on-screen like a wildly smart sportscaster. Stories also help audiences identify with a speaker, encouraging em*pathy* and sym*pathy* as audiences imagine, for example, what it was like for Tony Coelho to receive his epilepsy diagnosis (page 83) or what it felt like for Becky Blanton to find herself homeless (page 38). This is the persuasive power advocates tap into when they share their personal stories with audiences.

But pathos is only one type of persuasive appeal. Ethos, logos, and pathos work together. And effective communicators know how and when to draw on each in different situations and for various effects, rather than relying on any one appeal too heavily. For example, a speaker who depends mainly on his credibility (ethos) may have an impressive reputation and engaging delivery; but without presenting a sound argument or eliciting the audience's passions, he can appear hollow. A speaker who presents reams of data and an airtight case (logos) may be difficult to argue with; she may also be difficult to listen to for very long if she doesn't seem to care about the audience. And while someone's personal story of adversity can smack us in the gut (pathos), if we suspect that smack was the speaker's sole intent and we are left with nothing else, we may walk away feeling played.

That's why in *Living Proof* we emphasize that using a personal story as a tool of advocacy is not simply a matter of "Insert Story

Here." Personal stories—as powerful as we know they can be—should not be asked to carry the entire weight of a persuasive act. Doing so risks having an audience dismiss them as "just" stories, relying too heavily on emotions over reason, or presenting too singular a view.

The recommendations we make in *Living Proof* aim at helping advocates balance the considerable "pathetic" appeal of personal stories by drawing also upon the persuasive power of logos and ethos. Here are some examples:

Logos—persuading through logic and reasoning—also refers to the internal consistency of a message, its clarity, purposeful organization, and supporting material. Personal stories are most effective when they are linked to key messages, evidence, or statistics, organized strategically, and framed within a larger context. While a personal story can "put a face" on an issue, logic and reasoning give a personal story "legs." Pathos and logos are the one-two punch to heart and head.

RELATED CHAPTERS:
Chapter 3: Focus Your Stories
Chapter 6: Frame It
Chapter 7: Strategic by Design

The very act of sharing a personal story publicly can contribute to a speaker's **ethos**—persuasion that occurs by means of character or credibility. Think how often U.S. politicians—especially during campaign season—support a view or issue with a personal experience. Offering "living proof" of a message establishes a certain authority and expertise on a subject, and audiences typically respond favorably when a speaker draws from his or her lived experience and personalizes a message (predominantly in Western cultures, though not consistently).

But ethos is also conveyed in how an audience views a speaker's trustworthiness and integrity; if the politician's folksy family tale doesn't ring true, we can be just as quick to judge his attempt as condescending or insincere. Personal stories are most effective within the context of advocacy when spoken truthfully, honestly, and respectfully; when the advocate is transparent and clear about the advocacy goal and its benefits to the audience; when the story is framed clearly in terms of what it is and what it is not.

Finally, ethos is also conveyed through tone, voice, and style of speaking. Advocates who are clear, concise, organized, comfortable, and confident, whether speaking on a street corner or on national television, build credibility with their audiences.

===

RELATED CHAPTERS:
Chapter 3: Focus Your Stories
Chapter 4: Point to the Positive
Chapter 6: Frame It
Chapter 7: Deliver Powerful Presentations
Chapter 13: Public Speaking: Tips and Tools

===

Personal Stories and Social Change

L iving Proof is grounded in the belief that shared life experiences have the potential to move audiences from apathy to empathy to action. Our focus is on the individual advocate and what it takes for one person's story to become a powerful, persuasive tool of positive change.

But individual advocacy doesn't happen in a vacuum. While individual advocates are making a difference in their corners of the world—helping to increase awareness and understanding, encourage participation, change attitudes, behaviors, laws, or policies—coalitions and networks are working simultaneously to create change at broader institutional, community, national, or international levels. Picture it: one advocate tells a story—Zach Wahls stands before Iowa legislators giving proof that loving families come in all forms; Theresa Greenleaf sits with other parents in a grade school library giving proof that children with food allergies need protections…

Meanwhile, like-minded advocates are coming together to marshal resources and gather evidence. Grass-roots support is growing. Partnerships and coalitions are being built at local, regional, and national levels. Communities are organizing and organizations are strengthening. Lobbyists and strategists are working to ensure messages reach the media or the desks of legislators. Corporations, foundations, religious institutions, and individuals are allocating dollars. Artists and activists make public statements. Celebrities and high-level champions take the stage. Tweets fly, posts are liked, videos go viral …

The marvel of any successful social movement is that these efforts and voices manage to coalesce: the personal stories being told at state legislatures and in grade school libraries link to the larger narratives being written collectively and culturally. The story of one becomes the story of many—and the many make the difference.

This progression—from self to other to action—is at the heart of "public narrative," the story-based leadership practice taught by Marshall Ganz, professor at the Harvard Kennedy School of Government. Ganz's approach to leading change provides a way of understanding how individual stories and single acts of advocacy must link to and support broader efforts. His visionary approach has helped leaders and organizations around the world advance their causes.[8]

Ganz worked as an organizer in the civil rights movement in the 1960s, then with the United Farm Workers in California. He developed his public narrative principles from his experiences in the field, but the questions at the core of his pedagogy are rooted in his faith tradition and years of celebrating Passover Seders. He writes, "As Rabbi Hillel, the 1st Century Jerusalem sage put it, 'If I

> "Effective social movements often begin when once silenced people resolve to tell their own stories. In different ways, under widely varying circumstances, they state, in effect, 'this is who I am. This is how my community's hopes and dreams have systematically been spurned and destroyed. And this is how things have to change.' Through the telling of these stories, people learn to view their lives as intertwined with history."[7]
>
> **—Paul Rogat Loeb**

am not for myself, who will be for me? If I am for myself alone, what am I? If not now, when?""[9] Built upon these foundational questions, public narrative is a fusion of three elements: the Story of Self, the Story of Us, and the Story of Now. Ganz's descriptions of these three narratives resonate deeply with key themes that run through *Living Proof*, and his approach provides an inspirational and strategic means of leveraging the power of individual advocacy stories.

The Story of Self

"A Story of Self communicates the values that call one to action" (Ganz, p. 14).[10] Story of Self is the primary focus of *Living Proof*— telling a story that has its roots in lived experience, in support of a cause—and we begin the book with the question we ask advocates at the start of all our workshops: Why are you an advocate? This is the essential starting place of meaningful individual advocacy; being able to articulate the *why* provides a foundation that grounds advocates throughout the process of deciding what to tell, crafting stories, linking stories to key messages, preparing to speak, and then speaking out. The Story of Self provides specific, tangible, living proof of why we are committed to an idea or a cause. As Ganz explains,

> Telling one's Story of Self is a way to communicate our identity, the choices that have made us who we are, and the values that shaped those choices—not as abstract principle, but as lived experience. (p. 17)

We build our Stories of Self around key *choice points* we've made in our lives, naming the changes that occurred in us from Then to Now.

Throughout *Living Proof,* we give examples of how advocates convey their Stories of Self—and the values that inform them—with passion and conviction. One such illustration is the presentation given by Scott Harrison, founder of charity: water, at the Big Omaha tech conference. By starting with his Story of Self, Scott demonstrates how he—a former fast-living nightclub promoter—ended up being the guy who started an organization dedicated to bringing clean drinking water to developing countries. He relates key choice points: rebelling against his church, returning to his faith, and deciding to join Mercy Ships, where he took his first trip to Liberia and saw thousands of families needing medical assistance:

It made me angry. It made me want to do something with my life to help them… I realized what a mess I'd made of my life, and decided to come back to New York and really try to live out what I'd never stopped believing…

From his Story of Self, Scott moves to a Story of Us.

RELATED CHAPTERS:
Chapter 1: My Six-Word Reason
Chapter 2: Story Map
Chapter 3: Focus on Your Goals and Your Audience
Chapter 4: The Positive Change in You
Chapter 6: Build Your Frames

The Story of Us

"A Story of Us communicates the values shared by those in action" (Ganz, p. 15). The Story of Us demonstrates how the Story of Self connects to a larger narrative, one that encompasses and involves those in a community, organization, or campaign. When an advocate frames her personal story with statements that point to a collective identity ("As concerned and dedicated parents, we know that...") or shared values ("This is about taking personal responsibility for our..."), she alludes to the Story of Us. When the Story of Us is narrated fully, audiences understand the values they share, who they are as a community, and what is possible for them to achieve.

In his Big Omaha presentation, Scott Harrison congratulates the audience, reminding them they have already helped to bring clean drinking water to a community in Africa with the money they've raised and promising to "show you a little more of what that looks like." Later he demonstrates how "every two people here at this conference gave one person access to clean water" and, with specific stories and images of the people helped, builds the Story of Us upon shared values of equity, dignity, compassion, and charity. Later, telling how interest in his young organization began to grow as others recognized their own values being activated, he says: "Our 'why' was simple: *People should have clean water to drink*. That's it. Then other people got a hold of that 'why' and started doing extraordinary things." In his appeal for the audience to deepen their commitment, he finally asks, "will you make this your story?"

RELATED CHAPTERS:
Chapter 4: The Positive Change You Want to See
Chapter 6: Build Your Frames

The Story of Now

"A Story of Now communicates an urgent challenge to values that demands action now" (Ganz, p. 15). The Story of Now demonstrates that there is a clear and present challenge to our shared values, there is a hopeful choice each person in the audience can make, and that choice needs to be made right now. It is the need and the call to action, with a clear strategy, a specific ask, and a vivid description of what can be achieved.

After defining the severity of the global water shortage and the specific challenge facing charity: water (helping at least 1 million people get access to clean water by the end of 2020), Scott Harrison demonstrates the hopeful choices others have made to raise money, such as people "giving up their birthdays" to throw fundraisers, or "guys climbing mountains to raise $1/foot." While the task ahead is enormous, he demonstrates hope. He then gives his Big Omaha audience a direct challenge to get personally involved and to involve their colleagues, families, and friends. He closes his presentation by echoing the words of Rabbi Hillel: "If not us, who? And if not now, when?"

RELATED CHAPTERS:
Chapter 3: Focus on Your Goals and Your Audience
Chapter 4: Point to the Positive
Chapter 7: Strategic by Design

Ganz's practice of public narrative is one way in which leaders employ narrative frameworks to both understand and influence social change. The Center for Story-based Strategy, for example, also "provides a process to understand the current story around an issue and identify opportunities to change the story with the right framing, messages, messengers and creative interventions."[11] These broader applications of narrative only serve to remind us of the centrality of storytelling, at all levels, to the history and continued animation of social movements.

Leaders and change makers across a wide range of issues—from mental health to civil rights to the environment—continue to rely on individuals' stories to make the case for change. But Ganz provides us the important reminder that individual stories—and the advocacy of any one person—are at their most powerful when they are situated within the community and pointed toward positive action:[12]

> Crafting a complete public narrative is a way to connect three core elements of leadership practice: story (why we must act now, heart), strategy (how we can act now, head), and action (what we must do to act now, hands). As Rabbi Hillel's powerful words suggest, to stand for yourself is a first but insufficient step. You must also construct the community with whom you stand, and move that community to act together now. To combine stories of self, us and now, find common threads in values that call you to your mission, values shared by your community, and challenges to those values that demand action now. (p. 5)

Chapter 13

Public Speaking: Tips and Tools

IN THIS CHAPTER:

❑ Presentation skills reminders and hints
❑ Managing questions from the audience
❑ Prep sheets to aid in your planning

Delivery Tips

Selected Pointers and Guides

Staying Focused

1. **Focus the rush of adrenaline.** Remember your goal is not to *eliminate* nervous energy; it's to channel it in a productive way. Few things are more dangerous than going into an important public communication without any concern whatsoever.

2. **Be realistic.** You don't have to be perfect. If something goes wrong, remind yourself of your advocacy goal, why you are here, and the positive change you advocate.

3. **Repeat your advocacy goal to yourself before speaking.** Remind yourself why you're here and why you're speaking. Focus on the positive end result. Repeat your Six-Word Reason.

4. **When speaking to a new group, greet or speak to a few audience members beforehand.** You'll be guaranteed at least a few smiling faces and positive nonverbal support when you start to speak.

5. **Breathe.** Public speaking requires breath support. Mindful breathing also calms you and gives the audience time to process what you say. Plan spots in your presentation or talk when you will purposefully stop and breathe.

Managing Time

1. **Be realistic in what you can achieve.** Know your time limits and plan accordingly.

2. **Plan for less.** If given fifteen minutes, plan for ten. Audience reaction—whether verbal or nonverbal—adds time.

3. **Know where your timekeeper is.** Decide where you'll look to check your time. Place your watch or smartphone nearby. Find the clock in the room. Have a colleague give 10- and 5-minute signals. Don't worry about revealing that you are mindful of the time.

4. **Note your start time.** You may have so many things in your head when you begin speaking that you miss the obvious. Jot down your actual start time just before you begin, so you know how long you have. Also know what your stop time should be.

5. **Use technology.** Set the silent vibrating alarm on your cell or smartphone to signal when you're at the 5-minute mark. Some presentation applications, like Apple's Keynote, have great timers built in. There are also countdown clocks on most smartphones.

Starting Strong

1. **Shorten the run-up.** The *run-up* is the short sprint a high-jumper uses to gain momentum before jumping. It's also the time it takes a speaker to get comfortable in front of an audience. (Watch for it the next time you attend a presentation: you can see and hear when a speaker's body and mind relax.) When you begin, think of the speaker who normally emerges two minutes into your presentation. Begin with *that* speaker.

2. **Focus on one goal.** If you tend to have a quiet voice, make it your goal to start with strong vocal energy. If you have trouble maintaining eye contact, make deliberate eye contact from the very start.

3. **Make your first words strong.** The first words out of your mouth are the first words of your presentation. Plan them. If you begin with, "Um, hi. Okay…" this is how your talk begins. First words, like first impressions, matter—so make them meaningful.

4. **Pre-view the audience.** If you can, watch the audience before you speak. Position yourself where you can see them. Get a read on the audience's mood.

5. **Know your physical approach.** If possible, get into the space where you'll speak and practice moving to the speaking area. When you speak, confidently approach the speaking area. If sitting, purposefully sit up.

Using Language

1. **Avoid tentative phrases.** "I'd like to talk a little bit about…," and "What I hope to show you…" are examples of hesitant language about your topic and story. Used too often, they project a lack of confidence.

2. **If everything is important, nothing is.** Avoid repeating phrases such as "most importantly," "basically," "the bottom line is…"

3. **Use signposts.** Giving a presentation is like taking your audience on a journey. Point out what is important and where you're going next: "That's one reason we need this program. Another is…"

4. Avoid jargon or technical terms. Your audience may not be as familiar with the world of your story as you are. Be careful of using jargon; if using technical terms, provide definitions or context.

5. Reduce "verbal filler." Everyone uses an occasional *um* and *uh*. A few here and there aren't critical. But if frequent, they'll detract from your story and message. Practice inserting silence instead of "ums." With time, you gain control and can "turn them on and off." But be sure to work on this only during practice. Don't distract yourself by thinking about verbal pauses while you're speaking to your audience.

Using Your Voice

1. Vary your speed. Pausing helps eliminate verbal filler, and will help regulate a fast speaking rate. Vary your speaking rate to emphasize key messages and add interest. Breathe.

2. Pump up the vocal energy. You don't need to over-enunciate or be unnaturally animated. But think of using an energy level two notches above the audience's. Putting more power behind your voice will aid articulation, volume, and expression.

3. Relax and clear your throat. Before you speak, practice yawning, take a few long, deep breaths, or hum. Drink plenty of water the day you are to speak. Avoid clogging beverages and foods such as chocolate and milk. If you feel your throat tighten as you speak, pause and simply swallow.

4. Vary the volume. Find the appropriate volume. Can your audience hear you without straining? Or are you so loud the people in the next room can hear you?

5. Articulate clearly. You'll need to be extra crisp, especially if you have an echoing room.

Staging and Presence

1. **Look at the people you're talking to.** If you scan the audience or look away frequently, you'll appear evasive. Find the individuals in the audience.

2. **Make stance and movement purposeful.** Eliminate pacing and shifting. Plant both feet squarely beneath you. This will also help you project your voice and gestures more easily. But move when you have a reason to move. Transitions between sections of your talk, or before and after key points in your story, provide perfect opportunities to move. It's also a subtle way to help your audience follow the structure of your presentation.

3. **Cross-focus.** If you move to the right, look to the audience on the left. If you move to the left, look to the audience on the right.

4. **Show you don't need the lectern.** One of the most effective ways to use a lectern is to show your listeners you don't need it. Open yourself up to your audience by moving toward them, or stand to the side of the lectern.

5. **If using notes, don't hide.** While your goal is to speak improvisationally, at times you may need notes on an index card, a single sheet of paper, a tablet, or an iPad. Don't try to hide your notes, but be aware that they can distract attention. Practice with them. Look for somewhere you can set notes when you don't need them.

Managing Emotions

1. **Breathe.** If you become overcome with the emotion (whether sadness, anger, or giddy joyfulness), pause and take a few deep breaths before going on. The audience will understand and likely appreciate it; they probably could use a breather, too.

2. **Return to your purpose.** When you stop to take that breath, remind yourself of what you're doing and why you're doing it—the goals of your advocacy. It's also helpful to do this before you begin speaking as a way to focus.

3. **Reground.** A technique used by performers who find themselves losing attention is to make physical contact with something—the table next to you, a lectern, something in your pocket—and focus on it for just a moment. Because emotions can take us "out of the moment," contact with an object can bring you back. Then, breathe and continue.

4. **Name it.** It is sometimes necessary, even helpful, to let the audience know what's going on, that you're taking a moment to compose so you can convey to them your important message.

5. **Return to your positive change.** In the moment you take to gather yourself, recall the positive change your story and advocacy represents, and the better world you envision.

Speaking During Meals

1. **Time it right.** Whenever possible, speak with the hosts or wait staff to find out how the meal will be served. You often can schedule your talk while the least clinking and chewing is taking place.

2. **Change the seating.** If round tables are being used, ask that places be set on only half of the table so that no one will have to crane a neck or swivel to see you.

3. **Don't compete with the beef.** Delicious food can distract your audience from your presentation. Consider shortening what you have to say so they can get to their meals.

4. **Do compete with the beer.** Given the time of day, the size of the meal, and the availability of alcoholic beverages, your audience may be a bit drowsy or distracted. Recognize that your energy level may need to be punched up a notch, depending on these factors.

5. **Move.** Because there are so many distractions during a meal, and certain seating configurations may not be ideal, consider moving at times while you speak, positioning yourself in various places to make it easier for the audience to see you.

Using Visual Aids

1. **Know why you're using them.** Visual aids are just that: aids. They support your message, accentuate it, make it more memorable. If you're simply telling your story, consider whether you really need anything other than your own engaging delivery. Consider the physical space, the size of the room and audience, and sightlines when deciding to use visual aids. Large, projected images are appropriate for a large audience, but they may overwhelm a small group.

2. **Be prepared to do without them.** Ultimately, you are the talk, not your visuals. Plan to speak without them, and you'll be surprised how few you really need. You'll also be better prepared should anything go wrong with the technology.

3. **Practice.** Incorporating any visual aid—whether it's a slide show, video, prop, or handout—brings in another technical element to your presentation. Practice with the aid so you can use it smoothly and without distraction.

4. **Maintain control.** Every visual aid should have a purpose. If it doesn't or if it simply repeats what you say, omit it. Edit visual aids mercilessly. Realize that you don't always need to have a visual aid present. Take visuals away if they'll steal focus from what you're saying. Then bring them back as needed.

5. **Avoid pointers.** If you're using visuals, don't assume you need to use a pointer to direct audience attention. Pointers can subordinate your position by planting you off to the side of the screen. They also inhibit your gestures. Instead, try to close the gap between you and any visuals by moving closer to them and gesturing naturally.

Handling Questions from the Audience

A Four-Step Process

Your advocacy situations may occasionally include a question-and-answer session with the audience. Your mission during any Q&A is to answer as many questions as possible, while keeping the group focused on the key messages and your advocacy goal. Unless this session is being moderated by someone else, you may need to facilitate the Q&A yourself. In doing so, your role changes slightly from someone telling a story and delivering key messages to someone now facilitating a discussion. Aim for these goals:

- Clear up any confusion listeners have about your presentation or story.
- Prevent a single question or questioner from dominating the process.
- Draw links (see "Deflecting/Blocking and Bridging," page 160) between questions or answers and your story or key messages.

While there are no hard-and-fast rules for answering questions, this four-step process can increase the level of control you have over any Q&A session. Eye contact is crucial.

1. Give focus to the question and the questioner.
   - Listen carefully.
   - Establish and keep eye contact with the questioner.
   - Clarify confusing questions.

2. Pull focus back to the key messages of your presentation and story.

- Repeat or rephrase questions for focus and clarity, and so that everyone can hear.
- Identify issues when questions are controversial or unanswerable.
- Give eye contact to others in the audience (not just the questioner).

3. Answer.

- Keep eye contact on others in the audience (fight your desire to look only at the questioner).
- Be concise. Be honest.
- If you don't have an answer, admit it, but include a next step.
- Don't let the discussion stray into areas of confidential or personal information you've already deemed inappropriate for inclusion.

4. Give focus to another questioner.

- Keep the Q&A moving forward.
- Check back with the original questioner only if you want or need to. Remember that your responsibility is to the whole audience, not an individual.

Before the Q&A session begins, let your audience know how much time you have: "We have about fifteen minutes for your questions." Don't end the Q&A session abruptly. Let the audience know: "We have time for two or three more questions." Finally, when you have finished answering questions, repeat the main theme or key messages of your presentation and story, or repeat your call to action. This technique will bring closure to the process and reinforce your advocacy messages.

See "Handling Questions from an Interviewer" in Chapter 14 for more suggestions on managing specific types of questions.

Speaking Prep Sheets

Prepare for Your Audience

Demographic Information What ages are represented in the audience? What genders? Religions? Racial, ethnic, or cultural backgrounds? Does the audience represent members of a particular group or organization? What is the socioeconomic makeup of the audience? Consider language levels, appropriateness of content, culturally significant material, values and beliefs, issues of particular importance, and points of difference and similarity between you and the audience.	**Demographic Information**
Situational Information Why has the audience gathered to listen to you? Will the audience be aware of any other news, good or bad, and have it in mind when they hear you speak? Are they under internal or external pressure to listen to you? How large will the audience be? Is the setting formal or informal? Consider how your story relates to the audience's reasons for attending, the moods and attitudes they bring, their openness to listening, and their physical comfort.	**Situational Information**

Prepare for Your Audience *(continued)*

Attitudes Toward Your Topic What do they know about your subject, cause, campaign, or organization? What do they need to know about it? What do they want to know about it? What do they expect to hear? What is their level of interest in your subject, cause, campaign, or organization? Consider how you frame your story, any background information you may need to cover, what may surprise them, how you "hook" them, how you bring them new information.	**Attitudes Toward Your Topic**
Attitudes Toward You What is the relationship between you and your audience? What preconceived notions might they have about you? How much do they know about you and your experience? What information have they been given about you and your life experience? Consider how you frame your story, what background information you need to cover, what preconceptions you need to address, where you start your story, your physical relationship to the audience.	**Attitudes Toward You**

Attitudes Toward Personal Stories

How open are they to the idea of hearing personal stories?

With what level of disclosure is the audience comfortable?

Does your story go counter to other stories of which this audience is aware, or is your story familiar?

Has this audience experienced something similar to what you will describe?

Consider level of disclosure, how you frame your story as a story, what else you may need to include in addition to your story, how they may respond to the content of your story.

Attitudes Toward Personal Stories

Values, Beliefs, and Decision Making

What is important to this audience? What do they value?

How do they think? Upon what do they base their decisions?

What may they be skeptical about?

What will seem familiar to them? Foreign?

Consider what support you may need in addition to your story, what about your experience speaks to the audience's values, what may challenge their values or beliefs, what analogies you may need to "bridge the gap," how you frame your story.

Values, Beliefs, and Decision Making

Speaking Prep Sheet

Prepare for the Context

What is the speaking situation? What is the event or occasion? An informal meeting, outdoor rally, formal fundraiser? What is the ideal outcome of the occasion? What is it about your story that you or the organizers hope it will add to the event? What will the general mood of the situation be? Solemn, energized, tense, supportive, celebratory? Consider how you frame your story appropriately for the context, what you may need to acknowledge or address in addition to telling your story, whether the stories you intend to share are the best for the situation.	**What is the speaking situation?**
What is your role? Are you the primary speaker, or one of many? What are you responsible for conveying? Your experience only and its connection to the topic, or additional background information about the cause, the organization, etc.? How much control do you have over this situation? Is this entirely of your making, or is someone else determining the shape or agenda? What is your position on the agenda, if there is one? What happens right before you? Right after? Are you being asked to speak in support of particular messages, or is this presentation of your own design? Are there any regulatory restrictions on what you can or cannot say? Consider how your story or messages relate to other scheduled speakers, what information organizers may want you to include in your address, what key messages already exist that you need to link to your story.	**What is your role?**

Speaking Prep Sheet

Prepare for the Physical Environment

What are the details of speaking in this physical environment? Do you have 2 minutes or 20? How much of your story will you be able to share? How formal is the situation? What time of day and where will this occur? Consider how you scale your story for the time constraints, how you dress for the degree of formality.	**What are the details of speaking in this physical environment?**
Mode of Presentation Are there expectations as to how you will speak or from where (at a lectern, through a bullhorn, on a panel, in a circle, from a sofa)? Is the audience seated or standing? In the balcony above you? Surrounding you? What kind of audiovisual equipment will you need or be expected to use? Is a lectern available? Do you have to use it? Do you need a microphone? Can you get a wireless microphone? Are you speaking during a meal? Consider what the setting asks of your physical staging and use of your voice.	**Mode of Presentation**

237

Prepare for the Physical Environment *(continued)*

Potential Distractions	Potential Distractions
Is the audience's physical comfort (temperature, seating, etc.) adequate?	
Is the lighting appropriate and efficient? Can the audience see both you and your visual aids (if using them)? Can you see the audience? Is the lighting too dramatic, creating distance between you and the audience?	
What will be behind you as you speak? What visual distractions might there be for the audience?	
How are the acoustics? Does your voice echo, or is the room "dead?"	
Consider how event organizers might help you address any improvements to the physical environment or how you may need to alter your delivery to accommodate.	

Speaking Prep Sheet

The Basic Structure

Introduction
- Gain and focus attention
- Establish purpose
- Preview

Body
- Your story, or
- Your story and additional content structured around key messages

Conclusion
- Remind the audience of key messages
- Present them with a "call to action"

239

Speaking Prep Sheet

Story as Backbone

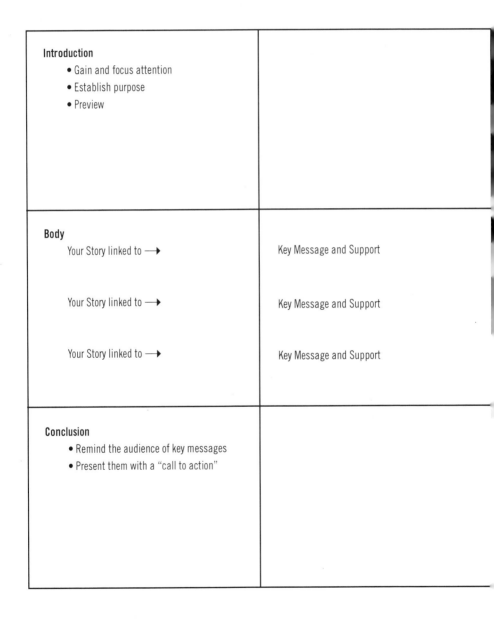

Introduction • Gain and focus attention • Establish purpose • Preview	

Body
 	
   Your Story linked to ⟶
 	
   Your Story linked to ⟶
 	
   Your Story linked to ⟶
	
	Key Message and Support
	
	Key Message and Support
	
	Key Message and Support

Conclusion • Remind the audience of key messages • Present them with a "call to action"	

Speaking Prep Sheet

Story as Proof Point

Introduction
    • Gain and focus attention
    • Establish purpose
    • Preview	

Body
    Key Message and Support linked to ⟶
 	
    Key Message and Support linked to ⟶
 	
    Key Message and Support linked to ⟶
	Your Story
	
	Your Story
	
	Your Story

Conclusion
    • Remind the audience of key messages
    • Present them with a "call to action"	

Speaking Prep Sheet

Story as Envelope

Introduction
- Gain and focus attention
- Establish purpose
- Preview

Body   Your Story...

            Key Messages and Support

            Key Messages and Support

            Key Messages and Support

            Your Story continued

Conclusion
- Remind the audience of key messages
- Present them with a "call to action"

242

Speaking Prep Sheet

Landing Points

Introduction • Gain and focus attention • Establish purpose • Preview	
Body Your Story linked to ⟶ Your Story linked to ⟶ Your Story linked to ⟶	Landing Point Landing Point Landing Point
Conclusion • Remind the audience of key messages • Present them with a "call to action"	

Speaking Prep Sheet

The Change Journey

Introduction • Gain and focus attention • Establish purpose • Preview	
Body Your Story: Where I Started ⟶ Your Story: Where I Am Now ⟶	Insight Key Message and Support Insight Key Message and Support Insight Key Message and Support
Conclusion • Remind the audience of key messages • Present them with a "call to action"	

Speaking Prep Sheet

Problem-Solution

Introduction • Gain and focus attention • Establish purpose • Preview	

Body
   The Problem
 	
   The Solution
	⟵ Your Story
	
	⟵ Your Story

Conclusion • Remind the audience of key messages • Present them with a "call to action"	

Speaking Prep Sheet

Brief, Brisk Blueprint

Introduction
- Introduce yourself and frame

Body
- Summarize your story
- Zero in on a powerful moment
- Link your story to the policy objective

Conclusion
- Make a clear ask
- Thank

Speaking Prep Sheet

Monroe's Motivated Sequence

Introduction
- Gain and focus attention
- Relate directly to audience

Need
- Make them feel the need
- Tell your story and support it strongly and vividly

Satisfaction
- Provide a solution

Monroe's Motivated Sequence *(continued)*

Visualization
- Help them see the solution working

Action
- Tell them exactly what they can do

Chapter 14

Media Interviews: Tips and Tools

IN THIS CHAPTER:

❏ How to prepare for any media interaction
❏ The special demands of different interview settings
❏ Common interviewer questions and how to handle them
❏ Prep Sheets to aid in your planning

Interview Tips

Selected Pointers and Guides

Striking the Correct Tone

1. **Be yourself.** Speak the way you normally do. Don't "try on" a new personality for the interview. You can best channel your nervous energy by forgetting about yourself and focusing on the value of your story. Reporters like talking to real people.

2. **Keep the interview focused on your positive change.** You may have to deflect or block a negative impression with a "No, in fact..." or "No, although...," but don't dwell on it. Move on to your story and its message of positive change.

3. **Deliver your story and messages with confidence.** After all, you know more about the story than anyone.

4. **Maintain your poise.** By maintaining your poise even when responding to the most off-the-wall or challenging questions, you present yourself as interested, helpful, and in control of yourself.

5. **Keep your interview attitude.** Wait until the interview is entirely over before you relax your interview attitude. Wait until the microphone and/or camera is off or the reporter leaves.

Using Language

1. **Make short, simple, and specific statements.** When you think you've answered a question adequately, don't feel

compelled to keep talking simply because the reporter has a microphone up to your mouth. If you're satisfied with your answer, sit in silence. Rambling may lead you to say the wrong thing.

2. **For edited interviews, pause after complete statements.** During the editing process, the reporter and editor will appreciate these breaks.

3. **Never speak off the record.** The reporter is always working, always gathering information, even when the interview is not taking place. Whether the interview hasn't started yet and you're having a cup of coffee and chatting with the reporter, or the interview is over and you're walking with the reporter to the parking lot, avoid off-the-cuff remarks or comments that might be taken out of context or inserted into your story.

4. **Use your vocabulary, not the reporter's.** Avoid repeating negative, inappropriate, or incorrect language (deflect or block it when necessary). While conversationally we borrow words and phrases from others all the time, in a media setting you don't want someone else's words to end up being your quote or sound bite.

5. **Manage the paraphrase.** If the reporter paraphrases your answers, make sure that not just the gist is correct, but also the wording. If not, correct it.

Looking Good

1. **Gesture comfortably.** Natural body language creates a positive impression. Lean forward in your chair and feel free to use gestures to emphasize and illustrate your story and key messages.

2. **Use color to your advantage.** For television or web interviews, avoid patterns that will distract the viewer; small prints and stripes tend to shimmer and strobe. Solid colors are safe bets. Avoid wearing all black (your head will appear to float) or all white (depending on your skin tone, it may reflect too much light on your face and wash you out).

3. **Look in the mirror.** For formal television interviews, make sure your socks are long enough to cover your shins in case you cross your legs and that your skirt looks as great when you sit down as it does when you stand up. Dangling and flashing jewelry is distracting, so keep it at home. Unbutton your suit jacket when sitting, button it when standing. Check your reflection for *anything* that might distract attention, from a logo on your cap to a speck of kale on your tooth.

4. **Be comfortable.** If you're being interviewed outside, dress for the weather. If you're being interviewed in a television studio, realize most studios are kept cool but can get quite warm when the lights are turned on. Mid-weight clothing or layers are comfortable options. If you learn that the piece is airing much later, wear something that will look right for that season.

5. **Be clippable.** If you'll wear a microphone, make sure you have something it can clip onto. Expect the sound technician to thread the wire inside your clothes.

Managing Emotions

See the section about "Managing Emotions" in Chapter 13. The same advice applies to interviews.

Closing Strongly

1. **Make the most of it.** Try to get the last word in (without interrupting), and make it your call to action or summary of key messages.

2. **Make your call to action clear and specific.** Say clearly what you want the target audience to do, and describe when and how.

3. **Include resources.** Provide one or two places readers, listeners, or viewers may go for information: websites, phone numbers, locations. In a print interview, feel free to offer more.

4. **Summarize key messages.** Remember to stress your key messages one more time. This is especially important if the interview has wandered off topic or gone on longer than planned.

5. **Thank the reporter.** Maintain the good relationship you've built.

Interview Settings and Dynamics

Making the Most of the Media

Interview settings can vary widely depending upon the medium, the audience, and the technology. Your interview may be for broadcast, webcast, or podcast, or for publication either in print or online. It may be an unedited conversation that makes your every word available to the audience, such as a live television interview or an online transcript of your Q&A with a reporter. Or it may be an edited piece, such as a newspaper article in which you're quoted once or twice, a promotional video in which you are one of many "talking heads," or local news coverage of an event that includes your 12-second sound bite.

Each of these settings presents unique dynamics you'll want to keep in mind. Here's how to prepare so you're ready to interact comfortably and effectively with interviewers.

Audio-Only Interviews

Your voice carries it all.

1. **Create images.** Because sound is the only stimulus for your listeners, remember to use the vivid language of lived experience to help the interviewer and your audience hear, visualize, and imagine your story. Paint a picture with your words.

2. **Sound your best.** The *uhs* and *ums* we use in conversation can make us sound inarticulate when we speak to the media. Replace these annoying sounds with a brief pause—

you'll give the interviewer and audience time to grasp what you've said and give yourself time to decide what to say next. Speak clearly and distinctly, using variety in your pace and inflection.

3. **Smile.** It sounds odd, but it's absolutely true: listeners can tell when you are smiling even though they can't see you.

4. **Use notes as needed.** Feel free to keep notes in front of you to remind you of key message points, facts, statistics, or organizational information. But if it's an in-person interview, be aware that the person talking to you from across the table can read upside down and may ask you about something you've written.

5. **When interviewed in person,** speak directly to the interviewer to maintain a sense of real conversation. When a microphone is in front of you, it's tempting to focus on it. Avoid this.

6. **When interviewed remotely in your home or office via phone or Internet audio,** create a space where you can take the call comfortably and with focus. Get rid of anything that might distract: other phones, televisions, incoming e-mail, texts, or call alerts, barking dogs, or curious colleagues. If possible, take the call standing; it will help you project your voice, sound more confident, and feel more in control of the interview. However, be careful not to create additional noise by pacing or to get distracted by something outside your window.

In-Person, On-Camera Interviews for Broadcast

You're always on.

1. **If the interview is not conducted in your home or office,** arrive early and take time to get accustomed to the environment. If you can, sit or stand where you'll be

255

interviewed and get used to any technicians moving around so you won't be distracted during the interview.

2. **Build rapport.** If possible, talk to the interviewer before the on-camera interview so you can get a sense of his or her personality. The interviewer may ask for a thumbnail sketch of your story or let you know how the interview will start. Mention some topics or points you'd like to discuss. Let the interviewer know you want to make this a good interview.

3. **Remember to relax.** You may be filmed from a variety of angles and shots, from close-ups to full-body shots and possibly even before your interview starts as a "teaser" before commercial break. Because you may not know what type of shot the cameraperson is using, look interested and comfortable even when you're not talking.

4. **Look at and speak to the interviewer.** Think of it this way: you are talking with the interviewer, and the audience (the camera) is simply looking in. Make eye contact with the interviewer as you speak and listen. Strong eye contact keeps you focused and projects confidence to the people watching you. Glancing away from the interviewer or at the camera can make you look evasive or uncomfortable.

In-Person Interviews for Print or Online Publication

You're (still) always on.

1. **Take your time.** There is no camera on you, no audience waiting for your next word. Just a reporter (on deadline) recording your information. After the reporter asks a question, take a moment to gather your thoughts before speaking.

2. **Expect the interview to be audio-recorded** (you may be asked to approve this), since it is helpful for the interviewer to quote you accurately.

3. **Use notes as needed.** Feel free to keep notes in front of you, to remind you of key message points, facts and statistics, or organizational information. Be ready for the reporter to ask to see them or ask you for a copy.

4. **Look around you.** The reporter will be taking note of your environment, attitude, and reactions for use in the story. If the interview setting is not neutral turf, think about what is around you and what else the reporter is looking at: framed photographs, cartoons on the fridge, notes on the table. What can you remove, restage, or adjust?

5. **The interview is not over until the interviewer leaves.** Don't assume the interview is over just because she or he has closed the notebook or turned off the recorder.

Direct-to-Camera Interviews

Whether your interview will be a CNN-style satellite remote or via webcam, the lens is your friend.

1. **Look at the camera.** Whether speaking into a television camera or your computer's webcam, treat the camera as a person. Maintain strong eye contact with the camera's lens, just as you would with an actual reporter. If your eyes dart or watch something off-camera, you can appear uncomfortable, distracted, or simply disconnected from the viewer. When interviewed via webcam, resist looking at your computer screen. If necessary, cover what's on your screen so you can focus on the camera.

2. **Present with your whole self.** While you may be in view from only the shoulders up, continue to move your head naturally to nod or speak. Maintain good posture and gesture naturally. This activity enhances the tone and emphasis in your voice.

3. **Keep your voice clear and engaged.** Part of your interview may cut away to images or graphics, and listeners may have only the sound of your voice to engage them.

4. **Be an active listener who's always on.** Use good listening behavior, as you would if you were looking into the face of a reporter. Assume the camera is always on you, from before the interview to several moments after you're confident it has concluded. Consider your facial expressions throughout the interview.

5. **If the interview is taking place on your home turf,** do a trial run with your webcam before the interview. Consider "the set" and what the camera can see behind you; check the lighting so you don't look washed out or in shadow. Position webcams at eye level or slightly higher.

Edited Interviews

Consider the editor.

1. **Don't overlap the interviewer's questions.** Begin your answer when a question is finished to give the editor a clean slice.

2. **Avoid saying the interviewer's name** or referring to a previous answer or discussion in the middle of a sentence ("...as I said earlier, Pete..."). While using the host's name in a live interview is appropriate, doing so in this situation makes it difficult to edit and may result in good information being left out.

3. If you are being interviewed for a highly scripted piece (such as a promotional video), be prepared to be asked the same question a number of times so that the editor has a variety of options to choose from.

4. Check in with the interviewer occasionally to make sure you're being understood and heard clearly.

5. If you expect to be interviewed for 10 minutes but know the resulting piece may include only one or two brief sound bites, make sure you repeatedly deliver what you want those sound bites to be.

Handling Questions from an Interviewer

Common Queries and Agile Answers

The questions interviewers ask you depend on many things: their knowledge of your story and cause, their attitude toward your topic, the amount of time they've had to prepare, and their level of skill as interviewers. Do your analysis of the situation to prepare for any questions you might get, and use the four interview techniques (deflecting/blocking, bridging, flagging, and headlining) to build your skills in responding to these common types of questions.

Type of Question	For Example	How to Respond
Closed	Straight yes and no questions. "Did you actually see this happen?" "The prognosis is really bleak, isn't it?"	Respond or deflect, then bridge to your story or message: "I did. And it just underscored for me the importance of . . ." "Advances have been made with treatments, and the good news is . . ."
Open	An open-ended question that is designed to elicit a full response. "What happened?"	Score! Take it where you'd like: go to your story, your headline, or your key messages.
Rapid-Fire	Several questions, one after another.	Choose one question and answer it; ignore the rest or return to them later if you'd like. "You touched on several points including what could be done to help solve this problem. The good news is . . . . . ."
Interruption	A question asked before you finish your point that steers you away from your story or message and on to another question..	Be polite. Acknowledge the question, but return to and finish the story moment or point you were making. "I'll come back to that question. What I was saying was . . ."

Type of Question	For Example	How to Respond
Darts	Negative questions that challenge: "How could you have been so irresponsible?	Refocus the question: "It's not really a matter of responsibility. Like many others, I was ill-informed . . ." Avoid using the negative language yourself.
Vague	Often from an underprepared reporter, these questions require you to provide a lot of background before you can get to your key message.	Score! Steer the interview in the direction you want it to go. Rephrase the question to make it more specific. "By your question, I think you're referring to the damage this kind of pollution can cause . . ."
Off-topic	Irrelevant or tangential question that leads you and the interview off track.	Deflect/block and bridge. "That's interesting. At tomorrow's rally, though, we'll be focusing on . . ."
Loaded Preface	A question that starts with negative or incorrect information. "As an organization for women with ovarian cancer, what kinds of programs are available at Gilda's Club?"	Correct the incorrect information in a positive way. "The great thing about Gilda's Club is that it's for anyone dealing with any type of cancer: men, women, friends, family. And the programs are . . ."
Impossible	A question you do not know the answer to.	Acknowledge that you cannot answer it, and say why. Offer to find the answer, if possible. "I'm not a scientist, so I can't answer that question, though I know someone at the Center who could. But what I can tell you is . . ."
Gut-Punch	A question designed to engage your emotions. "Can you tell me what it felt like when you first got the news of his death?"	Look to your emotional preparation and what you feel you can safely and honestly say while maintaining focus on your goal. Answer and bridge, or deflect and bridge: "It felt like my world had ended. But of course it didn't. So, two months later . . ." "It was really hard, but what I now realize is . . ."

261

Interview Prep Sheets

Prepare for Your Audience

Demographic Information

What ages are represented in the target audience?

What genders? Religions? Racial, ethnic, or cultural backgrounds?

Does the target audience represent members of a particular group or organization?

What is the socioeconomic makeup of the target audience?

Consider language levels, appropriateness of content, culturally significant material, values or beliefs of a certain demographic, issues of particular importance to them, and points of difference and similarity between you and the audience.

Demographic Information

Situational Information

Why has the audience tuned in or picked up the magazine?

Are they passionately attentive or multitasking?

If broadcast, will the audience be aware of any other news, good or bad, and have it in mind when they hear you speak?

What are the specialties or concerns of the media publication or program?

What is the focus or angle of the media interview or story?

What led to this interview or appearance?

Consider how your story relates to the audience's reasons for listening to you, the moods and attitudes they bring, their openness to listening.

Situational Information

Attitudes Toward Your Topic

What do they know about your subject, cause, campaign, or organization?

What do they need to know?

What do they want to know?

What do they expect to hear?

What is their level of interest?

Consider how you frame your story, any background information you may need to cover, what may surprise them, how you "hook" them, how you bring them new information.

Attitudes Toward Your Topic

Attitudes Toward You

What preconceived notions might they have about you?

How much do they know about you and your experience?

What information have they been given about you and your life experience?

Consider how you frame your story, what background information you need to cover, what preconceptions you need to address, where you start your story.

Attitudes Toward You

Attitudes Toward Personal Stories

How open are they to the idea of hearing personal stories?

With what level of disclosure is the audience comfortable?

Does your story go counter to other stories this audience is aware of, or is your story familiar?

Has this audience experienced something similar to what you will describe?

Consider level of disclosure, how you frame your story as a story, what else you may need to include in addition to your story, how they may respond to the content of your story.

Attitudes Toward Personal Stories

Prepare for Your Audience *(continued)*

Values, Beliefs, and Decision Making	Values, Beliefs, and Decision Making
What is important to this audience? What do they value? How do they think? Upon what do they base their decisions? What may they be skeptical about? What will seem familiar to them? Foreign? Consider what support you may need in addition to your story, what about your experience speaks to the audience's values, what may challenge their values or beliefs, what analogies you may need to "bridge the gap," how you frame your story.	

Interview Prep Sheet

Prepare for the Context

What is the media situation? What is the reason for the interview? Why are you being interviewed at this time? Is it in response to other news, the time of year, a controversy arising, an upcoming event, or general interest? What is the focus or angle of this story? Are there other people the interviewer may have spoken to for the story? What kind of deadline is the interviewer under? Consider how your subject or story relates to the target audience's interest in and reasons for listening to you, whether there may be questions regarding other news or events, what the best version of your story is to tell.	**What is the media situation?**
Your Role Are you the sole interviewee or one of many? What do you want to convey? Your story only or background information about the cause or the organization? Prepare the specific key messages you need to convey in the interview, and practice any additional information you may be responsible for; research other potential interviewees.	**Your Role**

Prepare for the Context *(continued)*

What are the details of the interview? How long will the interview be? Is it TV or radio broadcast, online, print, newspaper, or magazine? Is it live or taped, edited or unedited? In studio, on location, sitting or standing? Telephone? Via the Internet? Are there expectations about the degree of formality or what you are to wear? Practice fitting your story and messages to the appropriate time frame; look to "Interview Settings and Dynamics" (page 254) for help with particular media forms.	**What are the details of the interview?**
The Interviewer How familiar is the reporter with your cause? Does she or he have preconceived ideas or biases? Based on what you've seen, heard, or read of the interviewer's other work, what type of questions does he or she ask? Does the interviewer seem prepared? New to the job or seasoned? What tone can you expect from this interviewer regarding his or her support of your cause? Write and practice answering questions you might expect from this interviewer; know the first message or headline you want to stress and what call to action you want to end with.	**The Interviewer**

Notes

Introduction to the Expanded Edition

1. Our thanks to the advocates quoted throughout *Living Proof*: Becky Blanton, Kristin Brumm, Majora Carter, Carey Christensen, Derek Cotton, Glenton Davis, Theresa Greenleaf, Scott Harrison, LeDerick Horne, Drake Larsen, Kathy Kastan, Teresa Opheim, Gayathri Ramprasad, Ocean Robbins, Lawrence Stallworth II, Loren Vaillancourt, and Zach Wahls. Unless otherwise noted, quotes are taken from personal interviews conducted by the authors.

2. Mary Pipher, *Writing to Change the World* (New York: Riverhead, 2006), 13.

Chapter 1 Your Stories as Living Proof

1. Katie L. Roeger, Amy S. Blackwood, and Sarah L. Pettijohn, *The Nonprofit Almanac 2012* (Washington, DC: Urban Institute Press, 2012).

2. "To Increase Charitable Donations, Appeal to the Heart—Not the Head," Knowledge@Wharton, June 27, 2007 (Philadelphia: University of Pennsylvania).

3. Marshall Ganz, "Leading Change: Leadership, Organization, and Social Movements," in *Handbook of Leadership Theory and Practice: A Harvard Business School Centennial Colloquium*, eds. Nitin Nohria and R. Khurana (Danvers, CT: Harvard Business School Press, 2010), 15–16.

4. Sheri Ledbetter. "What Americans Fear Most—New Poll from Chapman University." *Chapman University Press Room*. October 20, 2014. (https://blogs.chapman.edu/press-room/2014/10/20/what-americans-fear-most-new-poll-from-chapman-university/).

Chapter 2 Map Your Experience

1. Mary Pipher, *Writing to Change the World* (New York: Riverhead, 2006), 46.

2. Becky Blanton, "The Year I Was Homeless," TED Global Conference, filmed July 2009.

3. Tim Russert, ed., *Wisdom of Our Fathers: Lessons and Letters from Daughters and Sons* (New York: Random House, 2006).

4. Jack Maguire, *The Power of Personal Storytelling: Spinning Tales to Connect with Others* (New York: J.P. Tarcher/Putnam, 1998), 54–55.

5. Shirley Jackson, "Experience and Fiction," in *Come along with Me: Part of a Novel, Sixteen Stories, and Three Lectures*, ed. S. E. Hyman (New York: Penguin Books, 1968), 199.

6. Maguire, *The Power of Personal Storytelling*, 58.

Chapter 3 Focus Your Stories

1. John Elder, quoted in *The Story Handbook: A Primer on Language and Storytelling for Land Conservationists*, ed. Helen Whybrow (White River Junction, VT: Chelsea Green Publishing, 2003), 79.

2. Roger C. Schank, *Tell Me a Story: Narrative and Intelligence* (Evanston, IL: Northwestern University Press, 1995), 12.

3. Tristine Rainer, *Your Life as Story: Discovering The "New Autobiography" and Writing Memoir as Literature* (New York: Jeremy P. Tarcher/Putnam, 1998), 47.

Chapter 4 Point to the Positive

1. Gayathri Ramprasad, *Shadows in the Sun: Healing from Depression and Finding the Light Within.* (Center City, MN: Hazelden Publishing, 2014).

2. Becky Blanton, "The Year I Was Homeless," TED Global Conference, filmed July 2009.

Chapter 5 Craft Your Story

1. Robert McKee, *Story: Substance, Structure, Style and the Principles of Screenwriting* (New York: HarperCollins, 1997), 27.

2. Tony Coelho, Testimony during the Hearing on Discrimination on the Basis of Disability at the Joint House/Senate Hearings on the ADA, Washington, D.C., September 27, 1988.

3. Jack Maguire, *The Power of Personal Storytelling: Spinning Tales to Connect with Others* (New York: J.P. Tarcher/Putnam, 1998).

4. Tami Spry, *Body, Paper, Stage: Writing and Performing Autoethnography* (Walnut Creek, CA: Left Coast Press, 2011), 19.

5. Mary Pipher, *Writing to Change the World* (New York: Riverhead, 2006), 119.

6. Majora Carter, "Greening the Ghetto," TED Global Conference, filmed June 2006.

Chapter 6 Frame It

1. George Lakoff, *Don't Think of an Elephant! Know Your Values and Frame the Debate: The Essential Guide for Progressives* (White River Junction, VT: Chelsea Green Publishing, 2004), p. xv.

2. Robert Gardner, "Identity Frames," in *Beyond Intractability*, eds. Guy Burgess and Heidi Burgess. Conflict Information Consortium of the University of Colorado, Boulder, June 2003 (www.beyondintractability. org/essay/identity-frames).

3. Arthur W. Frank, *The Wounded Storyteller: Body, Illness, and Ethics* (Chicago: University of Chicago Press, 1997), 53.

4. Zach Wahls, "Zach Wahls Speaks About Family." *YouTube*, filmed February 1, 2011.

Chapter 7 Deliver Powerful Presentations

1. Margaret Mead, *An Anthropologist at Work: Writings of Ruth Benedict* (Santa Barbara, CA: Greenwood Press, 1977; reprint), xv.

2. Scott Harrison, "The Story of charity: water by Founder Scott Harrison," charity: water.org, filmed September 2010.

Chapter 10 Where Stories Lead

1. Zach Wahls and Bruce Littlefield, *My Two Moms: Lessons of Love, Strength, and What Makes a Family* (New York: Gotham, 2012).

Chapter 11 Moving from Silence to Story

1. Paul Rogat Loeb, *Soul of a Citizen: Living with Conviction in Challenging Times* (New York: St. Martin's Griffin, 2010), 34.

2. Tami Spry, *Body, Paper, Stage: Writing and Performing Autoethnography* (Walnut Creek, CA: Left Coast Press, 2011), 125.

3. Quoted in Helen Whybrow, ed. *The Story Handbook: A Primer on Language and Storytelling for Land Conservationists* (White River Junction, VT: Chelsea Green Publishing, 2003).

Chapter 12 Public Speech, Public Narrative

1. Matthew Bunson, *A Dictionary of the Roman Empire* (New York: Oxford University Press, 1991), 5.

2. *Political Dictionary*, Volume I. (London: Charles Knight and Co., 1845), 43.

3. Wayne C. Booth, *College Composition and Communication* 14, no. 3 (1963): 139–145. Toward a New Rhetoric: Annual Meeting, Los Angeles, California, October 1963.

4. "350.org Workshops: Telling Your Story." *350.org Workshops*, March 1, 2015 (http://workshops.350.org/toolkit/story/).

5. Sonja K. Foss and Karen A. Foss, *Inviting Transformation: Presentational Speaking for a Changing World* (Prospect Heights, IL: Waveland, 2011). Foss and Foss offer helpful distinctions between altruistic forms of rhetoric that intend to change the behavior of others (conversion rhetoric) or assist in making lives better (benevolent rhetoric) and "invitational" rhetoric, in which the communicator invites the audience to see the world as he or she does (p. 9).

6. Francesca Polletta, *It Was like a Fever: Storytelling in Protest and Politics* (Chicago: University of Chicago Press, 2006), xi.

7. Paul Rogat Loeb, *Soul of a Citizen: Living with Conviction in Challenging Times* (New York: St. Martin's Griffin, 2010), 34.

8. For example, 350.org builds its "toolbox" for climate activists upon public narrative principles (http://workshops.350.org/toolkit/story/).

9. Marshall Ganz, "What Is Public Narrative?" course outline (Boston: Harvard University, Kennedy School of Government, 2011).

10. Subsequent quotes are from Nitin Nohria and Rakesh Khurana, eds., "Leading Change: Leadership, Organization, and Social Movements," excerpted from *Handbook of Leadership Theory and Practice: A Harvard Business School Centennial Colloquium* (Boston: Harvard Business Press, 2010).

11. Center for Story-Based Strategy, "Harnessing the Power of Narrative for Social Change" (www.storybasedstrategy.org/harnessing-the-power-of-narrative.html).

12. Center for Public Leadership 2014 Public Narrative Workshop, Participant Guide. Originally adapted from the works of Marshall Ganz at Harvard University; modified by Kate B. Hilton.

Bibliography

For more information about the advocates in *Living Proof*,
and to access additional resources, visit www.livingproofadvocacy.com

350.org Workshops (2015). "3: Telling your story." *350.org Workshops*. Retrieved March 2015 from http://workshops.350.org/toolkit/story.

Alva, Eric. (2008, July 23). "Don't ask, don't tell: Telling my story to Congress." *TheHuffingtonPost.com*. Retrieved March 2010 from TheHuffingtonPost.com.

Blanton, Becky. (2009, July). "The year I was homeless," *TedTALKS*. TED Conferences, LLC, Retrieved March 2011 from https://ted.com /talks/becky_blanton_the_year_I_was_homeless/transcript.

Booth, Wayne C. (1963). "The rhetorical stance." *College Composition and Communication* 14 (3): 139–45.

Bunson, Matthew. (1991). *A Dictionary of the Roman Empire*. New York: Oxford University Press, 1991.

Carter, Majora. (2006, June). "Greening the Ghetto." *TedTALKS*. TED Conferences, LLC, Retrieved March 2010 from https://ted.com /talks/majora_carter_greening_the_ghetto_transcript.

Coelho, Tony. (1988, September). Testimony during the Hearing on Discrimination on the Basis of Disability at the Joint House/Senate Hearings on the ADA. Washington, D.C., September 27, 1988.

Fershleiser, Rachel, and Larry Smith, eds. (2008). *Not Quite What I Was Planning: Six-word Memoirs by Writers Famous and Obscure*. New York: Harper.

Foss, Sonja K., and Karen A. Foss. (2011). *Inviting Transformation: Presentational Speaking for a Changing World*. Prospect Heights, IL: Waveland.

Frameworks Institute. (2009). "Strategic Frame Analysis™ approach: Disciplinary influences." Retrieved from http://www.frameworksinstitute.org/sfa/pdf/disciplinaryinfluences.pdf.

Frank, Arthur W. *The Wounded Storyteller: Body, Illness, and Ethics.* Chicago: University of Chicago Press, 1997. Print.

Ganz, Marshall. (2010). "Leading change: Leadership, organization, and social movements," in *Handbook of Leadership Theory and Practice: A Harvard Business School Centennial Colloquium,* eds. Nitin Nohria and R. Khurana. Danvers, CT: Harvard Business School Press.

Ganz, Marshall. (2011). "What is public narrative?" Course outline. Boston: Harvard University, Kennedy School of Government.

Gardner, Robert. (2003, June). "Identity frames | Beyond intractability." *Identity Frames | Beyond Intractability.* Conflict Information Consortium, University of Colorado, Boulder. Retrieved March 1, 2015, from http://www.beyondintractability.org/essay/identity-frames.

Genette, Girard. (1980). *Narrative Discourse: An Essay in Method.* Ithaca, NY: Cornell University Press.

Gilliam, Franklin. (2009). "Vivid examples: What they mean and why you should be careful using them." *FrameWorks Institute* issue 33. Retrieved from http://www.frameworksinstitute.org/ezine33.html.

Harrison, Scott. (2010, Sept.). "The story of charity: water by founder Scott Harrison." *charity: water.org.* Retrieved March 2010 from http://www.charitywater.org.

Hilton, Kate B., ed. (2014). *Participant Guide.* Center for Public Leadership 2014 Public Narrative Workshop. Adapted from the works of Marshall Ganz.

Jackson, Shirley. (1995). *Come along with Me: Part of a Novel, Sixteen Stories, and Three Lectures.* New York: Penguin Books.

Kastan, Kathy. (2007). *From the Heart: A Woman's Guide to Living Well with Heart Disease.* Cambridge: Perseus Book Group.

"To increase charitable donations, appeal to the heart—not the head." (2007). *Knowledge@Wharton.* University of Pennsylvania, June 27, 2007. Retrieved Sept. 27, 2011, from http://knowledge.wharton.upenn.edu/article/to-increase-charitable-donations-appeal-to-the-heart-not-the-head.

Lakoff, George. (2004). *Don't Think of an Elephant! Know Your Values and Frame the Debate: The Essential Guide for Progressives.* White River Junction, VT: Chelsea Green Publishing.

Ledbetter, Sheri. (2004, October 20). "What Americans fear most— New poll from Chapman University." *Chapman University Press Room.* Chapman University, Retrieved March 2014 from https://blogs.chapman.edu/press-room/2014/10/20/what-americans-fear-most-new-poll-from-chapman-university.

Loeb, Paul Rogat. (2010). *Soul of a Citizen: Living with Conviction in Challenging Times.* New York: St. Martin's Griffin.

Lucas, Stephen E. (2012). *The Art of Public Speaking.* New York: McGraw Hill

Maguire, Jack. (1998). *The Power of Personal Storytelling: Spinning Tales to Connect with Others.* New York: J.P. Tarcher/Putnam.

McKee, Robert. (1997). *Story: Substance, Structure, Style and the Principles of Screenwriting.* New York: HarperCollins.

Mead, Margaret. (1997). *An Anthropologist at Work: Writings of Ruth Benedict.* Santa Barbara, CA: Greenwood Press (reprint).

National Meningitis Foundation. (2010). "Read Others' Stories." Retrieved Sept. 24, 2011, from http://www.musa.org.

Pipher, Mary. (2006). *Writing to Change the World.* New York: Riverhead.

Political Dictionary, Volume I. (1845). London: Charles Knight and Co..

Polletta, Francesca. (2006). *It Was like a Fever: Storytelling in Protest and Politics.* Chicago: University of Chicago Press.

Radner, Gilda. (1989). *It's Always Something.* Sydney: Simon and Schuster.

Ramprasad, Gayathri. (2014). *Shadows in the Sun: Healing from Depression and Finding the Light within.* Center City, MN: Hazelden.

Rainer, Tristine. (1998). *Your Life as Story: Discovering the "New Autobiography" and Writing Memoir as Literature.* New York: Jeremy P. Tarcher/Putnam.

Reinsborough, Patrick, and Doyle Canning. (2010). *RE:imagining Change: How to Use Story-based Strategy to Win Campaigns, Build Movements, and Change the World.* Oakland, CA: PM Press.

Robbins, Ocean. (2009). Opening keynote, National Alliance for Peace, Washington, D.C., March 20–23, 2009. Retrieved March 2010 from www.oceanrobbins.com.

Roeger, Katie L., and Amy S. Blackwood. (2012). *The Nonprofit Almanac 2012*. Washington, DC: Urban Institute

Schank, Roger C. (1995). *Tell Me a Story: Narrative and Intelligence*. Evanston, IL: Northwestern University Press.

Spry, Tami. (2011). *Body, Paper, Stage: Writing and Performing Autoethnography*. Walnut Creek, CA: Left Coast Press.

Turner, Victor. (1986). *The Anthropology of Performance*. New York: PAJ Publications.

Vaillancourt, Loren. (2010, March 7). "Beauty queen takes on distracted driving." *CBSNews.com*. CBS News, Retrieved March 10, 2010, from http://www.cbsnews.com.

Wahls, Zach, and Bruce Littlefield. (2012). *My Two Moms: Lessons of Love, Strength, and What Makes a Family*. New York: Gotham.

Whybrow, Helen, ed. (2003). *The Story Handbook: A Primer on Language and Storytelling for Land Conservationists*. White River Junction, VT: Chelsea Green Publishing.

"Zach Wahls speaks about family." (2011, February 1). *YouTube*. Retrieved April 25, 2015, from https://www.youtube.com /watch?v=FSQQK2Vuf9Q.

Acknowledgments

M
any of the expansions in this edition originated in the
rich, challenging, and insightful discussions we've
had with readers and advocates since the original
publication of *Living Proof*. We thank those readers and advocates,
first and foremost, and remain honored to work with and meet
so many individuals who are advocating for causes we hold
dear. We're especially grateful to the advocates who generously
contributed their stories to this book: Becky Blanton, Kristin
Brumm, Carey Christensen, Derek Cotton, Glenton Davis,
Theresa Greenleaf, LeDerick Horne, Kathy Kastan, Drake
Larsen, Teresa Opheim, Gayathri Ramprasad, Ocean Robbins,
Lawrence Stallworth II, Loren Vaillancourt, and Zach Wahls.
The following organizations contributed instructive examples
of story advocacy: charity: water, Gilda's Club Twin Cities,
WomenHeart: The National Coalition for Women with Heart
Disease, the National Meningitis Association, and Practical
Farmers of Iowa.

We also want to repeat our thanks to all those who made
Living Proof possible in the first place: mentors and colleagues
Beverly Long Chapin, Martha Nell Hardy, Dennis Beagen,
Annette Martin, Ron Pelias, and Jim Van Oosting. Thanks also
to Mr. Ries and Ms. Seegers (Richard and Deborah Lee) for
teaching generations of junior high and high school students to be
passionate about communication.

An amazingly talented community of storytellers and writers contributed insight and advice to the first edition, especially Irene Ziegler Aston, Cathy Camper, Joanne Gilbert, Robert Pela, and Rachael Quitta. Cindy Meier and Tami Spry provided smart, supportive and poetic words when we needed them most. Our network of advisors was extended greatly thanks to Maureen Burke, Renee Holoien, Holly Morris, and Dana Wilde. The expertise of fellow trainers and educators echoes throughout *Living Proof*; thanks to Poppy Gaskin, Dale Ludwig, Eddah Mutua-Kombo, Greg Owen-Boger, Elyse Pineau, Lisa Samra, and especially Jeff Bloch and Gail Quattlebaum for pointing the way down such rewarding paths.

The first edition of *Living Proof* would never have made it out of our heads were it not for a crack support team: coach Linda Strommer, first editor Laurie Walker and reviewers David Cohen, Sonja Foss, Loretta Kane, Nancy Loving, Gordon Mayer, Susan Raffo, and Leslie Shore. Very special thanks to Bev Bachel for sharp, substantive edits, for sharing her considerable knowledge of all things bookish and writerly, for enthusiastic pep talks and invaluable connections, and to Brad Norr for designing the look and feel of both editions of *Living Proof*.

Helping us shape this edition: The exacting eye of editor Christianne Thillen; advice and support from Jeff Bineham, Lisa Samra, and Jeffrey Sugerman; and, once again, Tami Spry—for frequently sitting next to us, literally, as we wrote. Thanks also to Jeff Bell and Sandie Dorman of the Adversity to Advocacy Alliance (a2aalliance.org) for introducing us to so many powerful advocates, and to assistants Kyle Carlson, Marlena Serviss, Carl Neblett, and Michelle Baker.

Finally, thanks to our dear cast of friends and family members who help us write the stories of our lives every day, and to Rob Kirby and Eric Nelson, the main characters.

About the Authors

Since meeting as classmates more than twenty years ago in a graduate school course about the power of stories told out loud, John and Tim have helped thousands of advocates and hundreds of organizations share their stories to increase awareness, educate, create change, or raise funds. Their clients are "ordinary" people and first-time speakers, CEOs, small and large nonprofits, and some of the best-known celebrities, media personalities, and professional speakers in the world. John (Minneapolis) and Tim (New York) join forces whenever they can to recapture the rapture of their graduate school days.

John Capecci, Ph.D. is a coach, consultant, and writer who helps nonprofits and corporations do award-winning work that touches hearts and turns heads. He's the owner of Capecci Communications (www.capeccicom.com), which he founded in 1996 after pivoting from his career as a communication studies professor. He provides clients presentation and media training, story development and coaching, and marketing communications. Frequently invited to speak on the communicative power of narrative, John also volunteers with arts, wellness, and neighborhood organizations, and is co-editor of a best-selling series of monologue anthologies.

Tim Cage is a communication trainer who's coached and consulted with award-winning celebrities and sports stars, business and thought leaders, clinical investigators, and everyday advocates who have extraordinary personal stories to share. Before launching Timothy Cage Communication Training (www.timothycage.com) in 1993, Tim was vice president of a worldwide PR/public affairs agency, and senior associate at an international communication skills training company. Tim is an original member and former chair of the University of North Carolina's Department of Communication Studies Advisory Board and has provided twenty years of service on the board of directors for Bach Vespers at Holy Trinity in New York City, currently as president.

Index

Living Proof Advocacy Training^{SM}

John and Tim offer one-on-one, small group, and multi-trainer sessions to advocates, spokespersons, and the organizations that rely on them.

There's no substitute for experienced coaching from a trusted guide who will ask the right questions, draw out the meaningful stories, and inspire confidence by teaching new skills.

- **Personal Story Development**
- **Presentation Skills and Media Training**
- **Media Interview Training and Preparation**

The authors of *Living Proof* are also available to speak at your event on the subject of personal narratives and advocacy.

For information, contact **info@livingproofadvocacy.com**

Visit us at **www.livingproofadvocacy.com**
Befriend us on Facebook—**Living Proof: Telling Your Story to Make a Difference**
Follow us on Twitter **@livproof**

Granville Circle
——— P R E S S ———
Communicating good ideas.

Publishers of
The Orderly Conversation:
Business Presentations Redefined

Dale Ludwig and Greg Owen-Boger

The Orderly Conversation is a groundbreaking resource for business presenters.

It offers a new approach to getting-business-done presentations—an approach that replaces traditional "public speaking" assumptions with practical strategies appropriate for the real world of business.

This book is for you if:

- what you've been taught about presenting doesn't work for you
- the strategies you use to overcome nervousness are ineffective
- you struggle to engage your audience when delivering prepared information
- you find yourself breaking the "rules" of visual aids because they don't meet your needs
- you struggle to stay on track once the presentation begins
- you feel that preparing and delivering presentations ought to be a lot easier (and less time-consuming) than it is

Read a sample or order your copy at **www.theorderlyconversation.com.**